THE POWER OF TANTRA MEDITATION

THE POWER OF
TANTRA
MEDITATION

50 MEDITATIONS FOR ENERGY, AWARENESS, AND CONNECTION

ARTEMIS EMILY DOYLE &
BHAIRAV THOMAS ENGLISH

ROCKRIDGE
PRESS

Interior and Cover Designer: Eric Pratt
Art Producer: Samantha Ulban
Editor: Adrian Potts
Production Editor: Rachel Taenzler
Production Manager: Jose Olivera

Illustration © 2019 Christian Papazoglakis, p.60.
All other images used under license Shutterstock and iStock.

ISBN: Print 978-1-64739-200-0 | eBook 978-1-64739-201-7
R0

This book is humbly dedicated to the Sacred One who dwells within.

CONTENTS

INTRODUCTION

You may think you know what Tantra is based on pop culture depictions that associate it with sexual gratification and the indulgence of the senses. However, that version, which is rooted in misrepresentation and cultural appropriation, couldn't be further from the truth. In reality, Tantra is a mystical tradition that has existed for millennia across numerous cultures. Rather than a pathway to physical pleasure, it is a profoundly liberating spiritual practice that gives us the tools to awaken energies within ourselves, deepen our awareness, and connect with all that is divine in the Universe.

We knew that it would be beyond the scope of this book to encapsulate every aspect of Tantrik teaching. However, within these pages we aim to provide a beginner's introduction to Tantra and meditative practices. We hope that the information here serves as a rewarding entry point to the traditions of Tantra—and possibly even as a stepping stone to seeking out a guru who can help you become a true spiritual practitioner of Tantra.

Our Tantra Journey

Before we dive into the teachings of Tantra, we want to introduce ourselves—Artemis and Bhairav—and share with you our own journey with Tantra.

The Tantrik path called to each of us because of its radical embrace of the sacred in everyday life. Unlike many other spiritual traditions, it does not emphasize the transcendental, instead encouraging an embodiment of the Divine. Tantra is more than a theory for us; it is a way of life. Tantra unfolds for us in every living moment. It is an integration of the sacred within everything we do.

We are not scholars; we are ardent and dedicated practitioners. What we share with you in the pages of this book does not come from academic study. It is wisdom derived from years of devoted practice, under the supervision of living enlightened masters. Tantra has brought us an overflowing fulfillment in and adoration for the unfolding miracle that is life, as well as a deep and profound connection with the spiritual heart.

In 2008, Bhairav learned of a humble and unassuming Tantrik master named Guruji Maharaj living in a small town in central India. Even after more than 10 years of traveling India on and off, Bhairav had never before heard of a living Tantrik master. The stories that surrounded Guruji were simple yet mysterious. Bhairav heard that this humble man was capable of astounding miracles. Compelled by curiosity, Bhairav decided to travel to meet Guruji.

Upon their first encounter, Bhairav was immediately struck by Guruji's clairvoyance, humility, and undeniable connection with cosmic powers. In one of Bhairav's initial meditations with Guruji, the Tantrik master was able to open Bhairav's *ajna* (third eye) *chakra*. At that moment, Bhairav knew that this was the master who would be able to guide him beyond his own self. After six years of studying with Guruji, Bhairav introduced Artemis to him.

Years of rigorous spiritual study and practice later, we received the blessings of Guruji to be facilitators of the Shivoham lineage. Today, we share its teachings at our ashram in the wilderness of Canada. Through this book, we hope to share some of this wisdom with you so that you may explore the deeply rewarding path of Tantra.

PART

ORIGIN OF TANTRA

This first part of this book unravels and unveils the mystical intricacies of Tantra. Together, we will explore a general overview of Hindu Tantra. Then, we will dive into its core principles and practices, unearthing the history, philosophies, and theories that underpin this ancient spiritual path. You will receive a foundational understanding to begin your Tantrik journey before you undertake the 50 meditations that follow in part 2.

CHAPTER 1

AN OVERVIEW OF TANTRA

Perhaps you're curious about Tantra but don't really know much about it. Or maybe you've read a little about Tantra and feel eager to start exploring the practices. Either way, this section will provide you with the basic knowledge and history of Tantra you need to put its teachings into action.

What Is Tantra?

The word "Tantra" comes from the Sanskrit root *tan*, meaning "to expand." Originally, "Tantra" was used in India to refer to spiritual texts, scriptures, and practices in general. However, this term has evolved over time and now refers to the spiritual system surrounding and inspired by a specific group of texts—a spiritual tradition, originally based out of India, that has existed for thousands of years.

The spiritual system of Tantra is rooted in the pursuit of enlightenment. However, many people also come to Tantra to improve their health, to find a suitable partner, to become successful in their career, or for other worldly pursuits. This can be achieved through various practices, one of the most important of which is meditation. Through these practices, a person is able to focus their mind, unblock energy centers known as chakras, experience a deeper awareness of the Universe beyond their everyday thoughts and sensations, and ultimately come to know themself as Divine. If any of this sounds confusing, don't worry. We'll explain each of these tenets in more detail throughout this book.

Tantra is practiced by people of various religions, most commonly Hinduism and Buddhism. The goal and philosophy of Tantra are the same no matter the religion, but the rituals and practices vary.

And even Hindu Tantra, which this book focuses on, isn't practiced the same way by everyone. There are different groups, called sects, that focus on different aspects of Tantra. A practitioner might feel called to one sect over another due to particular practices or philosophies, karma, personal history, or even just a natural proclivity. Within each sect there are also different paths, precise ways in which practitioners practice, conduct rituals, and perceive spirituality. We will explain the different sects and paths later in this chapter.

The Philosophy of Tantra

Tantrik philosophy is summed up in the expression: "What is here is everywhere; what is not here is nowhere." Put simply, all that exists and will ever exist, including every person and object, is one infinite Divine being whose body is the Universe and whose source is Consciousness.

Tantra believes that suffering occurs when we mistake our personal experiences for our whole selves. This causes us to be trapped by our identification with thoughts, feelings, memories, and sensations. The Tantrik journey begins when you start to perceive yourself as the infinite Divinity, not just your body and mind. Practices such as meditation allow you to turn your attention away from the distractions of the world and towards your inherent Sacredness.

If you are a *tantrika* (practitioner of Tantra), you can, with guidance from a guru, come to know yourself as the source of all and carry this awareness back into your human experience. In doing so, you can bring transcendence into everyday life. The world will become transparent and vibrant, and you will feel equanimous and peaceful, knowing yourself to be indivisible from both the material and the spiritual realms.

A BRIEF HISTORY OF TANTRA

Debated by historians and anthropologists alike, there's no one Tantra origin story that is agreed upon by all. This is due to not only the elusiveness of the tradition but also its oral beginnings. The earliest known written record of Tantra is within the *Rig Veda*, an ancient Indian collection of Sanskrit hymns composed around 1500 BCE. However, purely Tantrik texts were not written until around 500 to 600 CE.

While Tantra's exact origins are unknown, it is commonly believed to have ancient shamanic roots. From these beginnings, it evolved into a more fully realized belief system in response to oppression by the Orthodox Hindu society of India many millennia ago. At that time, many spiritual practices were inaccessible to ordinary people and strictly reserved for the highest Brahmin caste. By contrast, Tantra was relevant even to those not living the life of a monk, as it encompassed the extraordinary within the ordinary. Put simply, it was inclusive to anyone fueled by devotion and a love of truth, no matter their status in society.

This inclusivity established Tantra as a highly adaptable spiritual belief system that easily integrated into the other spiritual traditions of the region, primarily Jainism and Buddhism. While Hindu Tantra prevails in India today, Buddhist Tantra (commonly known as Vajrayana Tantrik Buddhism) has a strong following in Nepal, Bhutan, and Tibet.

The Divine Play of Shiva and Shakti

Tantra views the Divine as one reality made up of two indivisible aspects. We consider these two aspects to help us comprehend the incomprehensible, but in reality they are one. In Hindu Tantra, these two aspects are known as Shiva and Shakti.

Shiva, personified as the masculine aspect of the Divine, represents what is known as Consciousness or Awareness. Existing beyond all space and time throughout the entire Universe, Shiva is all-pervading. Shakti, personified as the feminine aspect of the Divine, represents the activating power and energy of the Universe. Together they are still and dynamic, Consciousness and energy, nothingness and everythingness.

While Shiva and Shakti are ultimately equal and inseparable, in some Tantrik subcultures, one may be considered more important than the other. These traditions accentuate one divine aspect to help the practitioner comprehend the *sadhana* (spiritual practice) specific to that path. Once a full non-dual recognition is actualized, no such distinction is necessary. These apparent opposites exist within every *jiva* (individual soul of a living being).

Shiva and Shakti are the figureheads of the two most commonly known Tantrik sects: Shaivism and Shaktism. However, there are many other Tantrik sects involving worship of a range of deities.

Across the various sects, spiritual traditions such as meditation, mantras (sacred syllables), *yantras* (sacred geometry), and *puja* (ritual) are practiced when worshipping deities, bringing about worldly and spiritual boons.

Shiva

"Shiva" translates from Sanskrit literally as the "Benevolent One." The early pre-Aryans of ancient India saw him as a Divine being who would shed blessings upon them.

Shiva is male-presenting and has a human form. However, this kind of humanization of the Divine should not be mistaken for the Divine itself. It is a symbol used to make the Divine more relatable and easier for the mind to comprehend. Ultimately, Shiva is neither masculine nor feminine, nor does he even have a body; his body is of the Unmanifested Universe, which is Consciousness without matter. Every soul and object in this world, both sentient and insentient, is made up of Consciousness. Thus, every object and being contains Shiva.

Shiva is the empty, vast, infinite space within which Shakti creates the world. It is from Shiva that Shakti takes form and cultivates the spark of life.

Shaivism is the term used to indicate traditions that worship Shiva as the Ultimate. Tantrikas who subscribe to Shaivism are known as Shaivites. For them, he is the creator, destroyer, preserver, concealer, and revealer of the Universe. Within Shaivism, there are many sects, and despite their differences, these sects are united in their love for Shiva.

Shakti

Shakti is known as Mahadevi (the Supreme Goddess) and is the immanent (or material) aspect of the Divine and the creative force of the Universe. She is all that is manifest and the fundamental energy that holds the Universe together. Tantrikas who worship

Shakti are known as Shaktas. Shakti is often presented as feminine, but this is only a cultural interpretation. Just as with Shiva, ultimately Shakti is neither feminine nor masculine.

While Shiva is associated with just a handful of characteristics, Shakti is associated with thousands. All of the manifestations of the material and subtle worlds are forms of Shakti. Without Shakti, there is no action, no manifestation, no life. While Shiva may be Consciousness, without life force (Shakti), he cannot be realized. This is reflected in the saying: "Shiva is a mere *shava* (corpse) without Shakti."

In Tantra Shaktism, the Das Mahavidyas (Ten Wisdom Goddesses) are among the incarnations of Shakti. They can be classified as benign or wrathful but always symbolize an aspect of Shakti.

Shaktism has countless sects, cults, rituals, and myths. Even though each order worships her in different forms, there is a shared understanding that they are all worshipping aspects of the One Supreme Goddess.

The Paths of Tantra

Within the multiple sects of Tantra, there are two paths: Vamachara (left-handed path) and Dakshinachara (right-handed path). These two paths differ in how they worship and to whom they are available.

Vamachara and Dakshinachara are distinct in their contrasting beliefs around purity. Vamachara is infamous for its use of the *panchamakara* (transgressive substances, also known as the "five Ms") in worship: *madya* (alcohol), *matsya* (fish), *mamsa* (meat), *mudra* (parched grain), and *maithuna* (sex). However, these rituals are often misrepresented and require traditional context to be accurately experienced.

Today, neo-Tantrik expressions of Vamachara through sexual practices are very popular in the Western world. However, the authentic Vamachara path is not so widely available. Only the most exceptional and extraordinary practitioners have the karma, constitution, and fortitude necessary to genuinely follow this path to enlightenment. Vamachara is considered a very solitary path because so few people are able to walk it and because it requires direct and constant observance from an enlightened guru. Vamachara is also considered a dangerous path because it is so alluring to the senses, which makes it easy to be misled.

Dakshinachara, meanwhile, strictly forbids the use of panchamakara. It is the more popular path because it is considered safer and easier to follow.

While the tools and energies used in Vamachara are heavy and dark, the tools used in Dakshinachara are lighter and more refined. It is because of this that students on the Dakshinachara path are not required to be constantly observed by gurus. All of the practices presented in this book are solely of the Dakshinachara path.

The Levels of Tantra

Kaula, Mishra, and Samaya are commonly understood to be the three main schools of Tantra. However, it would be more accurate to compare them to the levels or grades within a Vamachara or Dakshinachara path.

These levels all share the same fundamental belief system, but each has its own tools, practices, and rituals to aid in the path to *moksha* (liberation from the mind, also known as enlightenment). Many believe these levels to be mutually exclusive because, from the outside, they seem to be immensely different. However, in actuality, they are complementary.

To be clear, it is not as though you graduate and transcend one level for the next. Rather, each level may be drawn from at any time based on the practitioner's present constitution or the results desired. However, it should be noted that the levels are progressive and linear. Generally, Kaula involves external rituals, while Samaya is a more internalized, meditative level; Mishra is the intermediary between the two.

When beginning the spiritual journey, the practitioner often has a busy mind and requires more of the materialistic tools and rituals offered in Kaula. Kaula helps the unstable mind stay stimulated and engaged through these more external practices. As the practitioner gains focus, stability, and balance in mind and body, they will gradually move towards the internalized practices of Samaya. However, the practitioner may still need to use the tools offered by the other levels to complete a specific sadhana and achieve a desired goal.

Kaula — Family

Kaula Tantra involves external rituals that aid the spiritual practitioner in purifying and activating the first six chakras (which we will look at more closely in chapter 3; see pages 41 to 46).

The external rituals conducted in the Kaula path are preparation for practices in the other two levels.

Kaula practitioners raise their energy by building yantras (sacred geometric shapes), making *yajna* (sacred fire) offerings, or completing *samskaras* (mental habits), *kriyas* (purification practices), mantras (sacred syllables), Ayurveda (traditional Indian medicines and healing methodologies), and *asana* (physical postures). The Heart Kriya (see page 132) and Sanmukhi Mudra (see page 66) meditations draw from Kaula practice.

Though Vamachara practices are present in Samaya, Kaula is the level most often equated with Vamachara due to the externalized nature of the practices. Vamachara practitioners on the Kaula level in the Victorian era were shunned for their use of the panchamakara, which pushed Kaula rites into seclusion. As a result, Kaula initiation processes became exclusive and practitioners were pushed into hiding. It is this secrecy that makes Kaula the most studied, as well as the most misunderstood, of the three levels.

Mishra — Mixed

As its name suggests, the Mishra level is a mix of Kaula and Samaya. This mixing makes Mishra a kind of "in between" place, a blend of Kaula's external rituals and Samaya's internal meditations. The Mishra level is the preparatory phase before Samaya.

The Mishra path works towards sublimating the energies into the higher chakras. However, Mishra practitioners often use fewer external rituals and practices than Kaula practitioners.

Samaya — I Am One with the Eternal

The Samaya level is the austere and illustrious part of the Tantrik journey. Samaya empowers the practitioner to connect with the inner silence of the Divine instead of the world's outer aspects. Samaya is the highest Tantrik path, making it the most challenging.

Samaya involves the most prestigious disciplines that an initiate can receive on the Tantrik path: the inward chanting of mantras and silent meditation. It is through Samaya that the practitioner will eventually become independent from the guru and learn to rely on grace alone, maintaining awareness of the Divine and the Being as one. Through this blessing, the spiritual practitioner moves into Absolute Awareness, or what we might more commonly know as "enlightenment." As a yogi in the highest knowing, they are one with the Universe, and the Universe is one with them.

In part 2 of this book, you will undertake some Samaya practices that have been shared in Tantrik lineages since time immemorial. These will provide a taste of the Samaya level.

The Gunas

The *gunas* are the three qualities that create and bind the entire manifested Universe:

- *Tamas*: darkness and inertia
- *Rajas*: activity and passion
- *Sattva*: peace and purity

These gunas exist in everything, including that which is tangible and that which is intangible (such as our thoughts and emotions).

Everything in the manifest world has all three of these qualities, and they are constantly interacting with one another. Some
forms have more of one guna than another. However, this is only
understood when comparing objects; alone, an object cannot be
categorized by its guna.

Within all of the levels of Tantra, the gunas play an important role
in determining the sadhana (spiritual practice) and the tools used.
While the meditations in this book do not specifically mention the
gunas, you will intuitively begin to engage them as you work through
the various practices. This can help you cultivate sattva, soften raja-
sic urges, and work with tamas in the service of stability and rest.

In the sacred Hindu text the *Shiva Purana*, the gunas are
explained to be incarnations of three Hindu Gods, with Shiva
being beyond the gunas. The fact that Shiva is beyond the gunas
signifies that Consciousness, the Supreme Reality, is beyond form.
Shaktism understands the gunas to be the initial forms of Shakti.

In Tantra, there is a philosophical understanding that life continuously flows from one state to another, that we have no control
over how life unfolds, and that preferring one guna over another
only creates suffering. It is for this reason that Tantrik practitioners learn to utilize each of the gunas. Coming to the gunas
with a neutral attitude enables the practitioner to awaken to the
Shiva Consciousness that is beyond all form.

CHAPTER 2

THE TANTRA-MEDITATION CONNECTION

Of all the Tantrik tools, meditation is the most important. Through meditation we are able to activate energies within our bodies and deepen our awareness. This type of meditation differs from common forms of meditation practiced in the West, where the primary goal is tranquility and relaxation.

Tantrik meditations also differ in the way that they are practiced. Contrary to the stereotypical image of meditation with the eyes closed and the spine erect, Tantra meditations include movement, colors, and sound. Tantra recognizes the divine complexity that is life and therefore offers a variety of meditative practices, as you will discover in part 2 of this book.

In this chapter, you will learn more about states of awareness, how meditation and other Tantrik tools enable you to deepen your Consciousness, and the ways that Tantrik meditation enhances physical, mental, emotional, and spiritual well-being.

The Five States of Awareness

Awareness is a key concept in Tantrik practice. In an everyday sense, awareness describes how you perceive what's going on within and around you. However, in Tantra, the words Awareness or Absolute Awareness are used to refer to the essence of your being: that which is both beyond material existence and the source of it. Tantrik meditation can provide access to the basic states of awareness, Absolute Awareness, and the varying states between them.

It is commonly understood that there are three fundamental states of awareness we move through each day: the waking state, the dream state, and the deep sleep state. The ancient Vedic text *Mandukya Upanishad* acknowledges all of these states (by different names), plus a fourth state known as *turiya*, which is a state of Pure Consciousness that transcends the first three states.

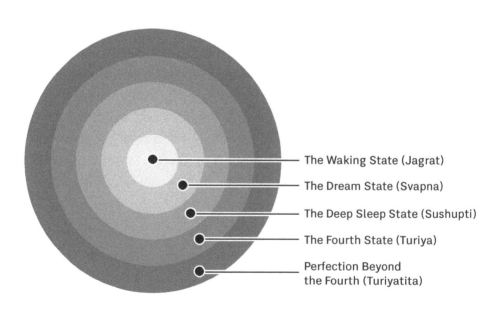

The Waking State (Jagrat)

The Dream State (Svapna)

The Deep Sleep State (Sushupti)

The Fourth State (Turiya)

Perfection Beyond
the Fourth (Turiyatita)

Tantra teaches that the fourth state's emphasis on transcendence limits a practitioner from integrating Absolute Awareness into their everyday life. Because of this, Tantra also identifies *turiyatita*, a fifth state that is both beyond and within all of the other states. In this state, a tantrika aims to dissolve their identification with both the individual self and the transcendent self and to merge the two into one Absolute Awareness.

In addition to moving through these different states of awareness, practitioners also advance through the five layers of self that surround the soul, known as the *koshas*. These layers are as follows:

- The physical body (*anamaya kosha*): If you feel a deep state of relaxation when practicing the meditations in this book, you are in anamaya kosha.
- The energetic body (*pranamaya kosha*): Meditations working with mantras, yantras, and Kundalini engage with pranamaya kosha.
- The mental-emotional body (*manomaya kosha*): Manomaya kosha focuses the mind and brings the ability to calmly observe emotions and thoughts.
- The body of higher intellect (*vijnanamaya kosha*): As you develop your discernment, intuition, and inner wisdom, you will begin to embody vijnanamaya kosha.
- The bliss body (*anandamaya kosha*): The cultivation and establishment of inner contentment comes in anandamaya kosha.

The Waking State (Jagrat)

Jagrat is the ordinary waking state in which you spend most of your life. In this state, you do everyday things and tend to perceive through the five senses (*jnanendriya*) of your physical body (anamaya kosha). For many, this is the most familiar and comfortable form of awareness.

However, you don't experience the full potential of your being when you are in jagrat. This is because in this state, Absolute Awareness has crystalized into an individual self that unconsciously mistakes its perceptions of the material world (which includes the external world as well as the internal world of our thoughts and emotions) for its whole self.

The waking state is associated with the physical body (anamaya kosha) and the energetic body (pranamaya kosha). It is also associated with tamas guna (see page 13).

The Dream State (Svapna)

When you sleep, you enter the dream state, *svapna*, during which your five senses are suspended. Awareness travels out of your physical body, moving through your soul to settle in the mental-emotional body (manomaya kohsa). In this state, you exercise your capacity for imaginative mental representation. This suspension of the senses happens unconsciously during sleep for most but can be experienced more lucidly by the experienced Tantrik practitioner.

In the mental-emotional body, you are not controlled by the desires of the five senses. You are instead under the influence of inner desires: will (*citta*), egoism (*ahamkara*), reason (*buddhi*), and mind (*manas*).

Although primarily associated with the mental-emotional body, svapna is also connected to the body of higher intellect (vijnana-maya kosha), as our dreams can reflect a higher wisdom beyond our desires.

The Deep Sleep State (Sushupti)

In the deep sleep state, *sushupti*, the two previous states merge. Here, there are no objects, experiences, concepts, or time. With nothing to perceive, we rest in the immensity of our being.

Many compare sushupti to a state of meditative awareness called *samadhi*, in which the jiva is absorbed in Absolute Awareness. In both states, the dreamer rests in the depths of the Heart. However, in the deep sleep state there is only ignorance, so the jiva forgets themselves and simply receives the benefits of restful sleep. By comparison, in samadhi there is awareness, and the bliss of one's Being can be enjoyed.

Sushupti is associated with the bliss body (anandamaya kosha) and sattva guna (see page 13).

The Fourth State (Turiya)

The fourth state, turiya, both transcends and pervades the waking, dream, and deep sleep states. While ultimately beyond words, turiya can be loosely defined as Absolute Awareness. It can be experienced through meditation, ritual, or any spiritual practice.

When we realize turiya, we have an awareness of our True Self not experienced in any of the first three states of awareness alone. However, because turiya pervades the first three states, it can be realized while still in any of them. It can also be experienced purely within itself.

Turiya in the waking state: When a person experiences turiya in the waking state, the jiva no longer identifies with the senses and the objects it perceives, instead achieving pure awareness as a witness to all things. Resting in the fourth state while in the waking state, the jiva finds peace and contentment regardless of external circumstances.

Turiya in the dream state: Many are familiar with turiya in the dream state from experiences with "lucid dreaming." In lucid dreaming, you "wake up" within a dream, realizing that you are dreaming and that the influences of the mind no longer control you. The mind is lucid, and you dissolve into the Absolute Awareness of the fourth state. However, this experience often returns to a semi-lucid state as you re-identify with a character within the dream and continue dreaming.

Turiya in deep sleep state: This is known as *yoga nidra*, or "yogic sleep." It is a form of conscious sleep, a state of awareness between waking and sleeping often experienced in the process of falling asleep. It can be induced by guided meditations, also called yoga nidra, in which the mind and body are laid to rest but awareness remains. In yoga nidra, awareness recognizes itself beyond the localized experience of the jiva. Since the jiva cannot exist in the deep sleep state, there is no sense of an individual self experiencing deep sleep. In other words, there is a subject but no objects.

Turiya in turiya: When turiya is experienced on its own, it is comparable to *nirvikalpa samadhi*, a transcendental state of awareness. Pure turiya is realized through the persistent withdrawal of the senses and focusing of the mind. In yoga nidra, there is a trace of inner awareness. However, in pure turiya, there is Absolute Awareness without subject or object. As stated in the *Mandukya Upanishad*, the pure state of turiya is soundless in the absence of the senses, fearless in the nonexistence of mind, and unutterable in the inability to verbally express.

When a person is experiencing turiya in any state, there is no desire; therefore, there is a cessation of suffering. The jiva rests, or completely dissolves into a non-dual state. Then a sense of Unitary Consciousness arises.

Perfection Beyond the Fourth (Turiyatita)

Tantra teaches that there is a state "beyond the fourth" known as turiyatita. To understand this, it is helpful to think of turiyatita not as a fifth state atop a hierarchy, but rather as the complete permeation of the first three states by the fourth until there is no longer any division between them. In turiyatita the Ultimate Reality is revealed and the entire universe appears as Absolute Awareness. With this realized, the tantrika knows that there are not three or four or even five states of awareness; there is only one. Final liberation and full awakening ensue.

It is this fully embodied and undivided Awareness that is unique to Tantra, as it does not aim to transcend the world but to awaken to the Absolute Awareness within everyday life. One who has realized the undivided reality of the world does not appear sub-lime or heavenly; one is instead indistinguishable from any other person and completely ordinary, as one's realization is grounded, embodied, and truly natural.

INITIATION BY A GURU

In both Shaktism and Shaivism, *diksha* (initiation) is one of the most significant rituals a tantrika can undergo. The word "diksha" is derived from the Sanskrit root *da* ("to give") in combination with *ksi* ("to destroy").

When a Tantrik guru gives diksha to a tantrika, they destroy parts of the ego and mental tendencies in the tantrika and replace them with spiritual knowledge or energy. Through the intention and grace of the guru, the practitioner receives the Shakti (energy) necessary to initiate and support their spiritual practice.

Doing spiritual practice without diksha is like trying to start a fire without a flame; it is possible but difficult. In the diksha process, the guru gives the student the flame of wisdom.

Tantrik Tools

Tantrik practice involves a number of tools. In fact, many Tantrik masters consider themselves scientists and use various tools to obtain certain effects among those who study with them. These effects vary based on the practitioner's intent and can include physical manifestations of good health, life changes (such as a happier marriage), and energetic and emotional shifts (such as a change in perspective or emotional stability). However, the highest objective of the use of Tantrik tools is to connect to specific energy currents (Shakti) to receive Kundalini awakening.

What is Kundalini? According to the science of Tantra, the human being is a mini-universe. All that exists in the cosmos exists within the individual. In this philosophy, the entire universe is a manifestation of Pure Awareness. In Tantra, we conceptualize this unitary Awareness as two aspects until we attain liberation and know them as one (see page 19). The first aspect, called Shiva, is unchanging and unidentified with the manifest world. The other, Shakti, is the creative force that brings forth the entire manifest world. Within the mini-universe that is your body, there is an aspect of Shakti that lies dormant at the base of the spine. This aspect is known as Kundalini Shakti, which is the essence of the Goddess's grace.

When this energy awakens, it generates an ascending movement of energy that rises through the chakras of the body to the *sahasrara* (crown) chakra, the abode of Shiva. Uniting Kundalini Shakti with the sahasrara chakra ignites Cosmic Consciousness. (If you don't know much about chakras, don't worry because they'll be discussed in chapter 3.)

The following Tantrik tools are used to realize the Ultimate as sacred and therefore must be employed with the utmost respect and reverence.

Asana — Posture

You may know "asana" as a series of postures that bring strength and flexibility to the body. However, in Tantra yoga, asana is used not only for strength and flexibility, but also to awaken Kundalini within specific energy centers known as chakras. The word "asana" can also refer to the simple posture traditionally used for meditation: seated on the ground with legs crossed. (It can also refer to any comfortable seated posture in which you're able to hold your body and mind still.)

Sitting directly on the ground, without back support, will amplify your meditation's benefits and induce a deeper state of consciousness. The steadiness of this posture aids the energies in their upward flow to the higher chakras. The meditations provided in part 2 contain specific instructions on the best asana posture for each practice.

In Tantra, "asana" also refers to the sacred mat that you sit on for meditation. This mat is made of natural materials and may contain various elements or colors depending on the effect you wish to achieve. Through repetitive use, the asana mat builds power and energy that supports you in your sadhana. The asana mat is used for every meditation and can grow to have a psychosomatic effect: In the same way that putting on pajamas and brushing your teeth might make your body feel tired and ready for sleep, getting out your asana mat and performing your pre-meditative rituals can help your mind and body slip into a meditative state.

If you are just embarking on your Tantra journey, using a synthetic asana is not a problem; you will still achieve many of the benefits that come with practicing yoga. However, if you're hoping to awaken Kundalini, it's better to use an asana made of natural materials, such as wool or cotton.

Mudra — Gesture

Mudra means "gesture." From a Tantrik perspective, every movement of the body can bring a different energy. Through the practice of mudra, we can understand the different energetic effects created by the hands, the body, and even the mind.

Mudra is most commonly a part of Hindu Tantra, but it is also found in Tantrik Buddhism, yoga, and Theravada Buddhism. Mudra can be a mere symbol, but it can also cultivate divine energies within the body and mind. Mudra in Tantra is used to awaken the energy within the chakras. In part 2, you will use mudra in various meditation practices.

Mantra — Sacred Word

One of Tantra's most powerful tools is mantra, which is a series of sacred sounds or words repeated to aid in meditation. Mantras can be in any language, but the tradition of mantra was initially passed down from the seers (Rishis) of ancient India and typically uses Sanskrit words. Sanskrit is an extraordinary language, as every letter of its alphabet corresponds with an aspect of a specific chakra. Using a mantra during ritual or meditation helps a sadhak (practitioner of Tantra) open cosmic energies and manifest the Divine within.

Mantras that you receive from a book do not have the same power as mantras that you receive directly from a guru. When the guru gives you a mantra as part of diksha, it is impregnated with Shakti.

However, with or without a guru, mantras awaken the divine aspects of the Universe that exist within the practitioner. Mantras can work equally well with the unmanifest of Shiva or the manifest of Shakti; they can be long or short, forceful or gentle. Mantras are very specific and must be recited appropriately in both *svara* (rhythm) and *varna* (sound).

A Tantrik sadhak must practice mantra with a process comprised of four parts: *japa* (internal repetition), *dharana* (concentration of the mind), asana (steadiness in the body), and *bhavana* (devotion). With each of these components implemented, your body will become like Shiva and the internalized mantra will be Shakti. Together they will form the Universe embodied.

In part 2, you will have the opportunity to work with ancient sacred mantras for healing, removing obstacles, awakening chakras, and finding spiritual realization.

Yantra — Symbolic Diagram

A yantra is a symbolic diagram of the Divine, but it should not be mistaken for a deity's direct representation. A yantra helps connect you with the Divine while also subduing the negative qualities and suffering that the Divine causes.

There are two types of yantra. One is an amulet that may be worn or kept in the home. It is often used for protection and can ward off harmful disturbances. Such yantra can be printed on paper, wood, stone, or any material, depending on the desired result.

To create the second type of yantra, you must follow intense rites and rules beforehand, then build the yantra out of particular ingredients. In completing this task, you will bring the energy of a specific deity to Earth through the empowerment of the yantra. In essence, the yantra becomes the body of the Divine, and you can receive the blessings of having close proximity to the deity invoked.

In part 2, you will work with a specific meditation called Trataka (see page 56) in which you will gaze upon a yantra to build focus and awaken energy. You will also do a more dynamic meditation in which you will practice drawing a yantra to encourage clarity and concentration of mind, as well as devotion and reverence.

Ayurveda — Healing Methods

Ayurveda is an ancient healing methodology that helps develop the body and mind to perform sadhana. If you are in poor health, a Tantrik guru may suggest a specific diet or lifestyle change or have you consume certain types of herbs or rub them on your body. These ayurvedic practices can be performed as a preliminary measure to prepare your body for the energy received in sadhana, or following sadhana, to hold on to energy developed through it.

As Ayurveda is a medical science, don't attempt to create your own ayurvedic prescriptions. Instead, seek the advice of an experienced ayurvedic professional for supplementary support and guidance in this area.

Yajna — Ritual Offering

Yajna can be translated as "sacrifice." Generally, it is a fire ceremony in which a deity is venerated through the chanting of mantras and the offering of a sacred mixture called *samagri*. Such oblations are regularly sattvic in nature and specific to the particular deity one wants to worship.

To perform yajna, you need to consecrate a physical space and build a three-tiered yantra, also known as a *kund* (in non-Tantrik practices, such a yajna only has one tier). Each tier represents one of the three gunas (see page 13 in chapter 1). Acknowledging and incorporating all of the gunas is key to Tantra, as it sees all of life as sacred.

Tantrikas consider yajna to be the most potent ritual, as it combines the making and empowering of a yantra with the devotion of *mantrasamagri* offerings. These two activities performed in conjunction establish the conditions necessary to receive the highest blessings. Yajna harmonizes the microcosm (the practitioner) with the cosmos's power (Shakti).

Rewards of Tantra Meditation

In this section, you will learn how practicing the 50 meditations provided in this book with dedication, persistence, and devotion can enrich your existence.

When a Tantrik practitioner perfects a particular practice, they obtain a *siddhi*. Siddhi means "perfection," and obtaining one often means you have developed the capacity for certain "powers." In the Tantrik texts, we read about siddhis bringing the power to levitate, read minds, see into the future, or even avoid death. These powers may sound mystical or imagined, but for tantrikas it is a simple reality that our sadhana can influence aspects of ourselves and the world around us.

It will be no surprise to the reader that siddhis are not obtained easily. Karmic influences, imbalances in the body, and lack of aspiration stand in the way of the practitioner's ability to obtain a siddhi. Obstacles can only be overcome with good intentions and a pure heart. The support and guidance of an authentic guru can aid you in staying persistent on the path, awakening siddhis, and obtaining the ultimate goal: enlightenment.

Physical Benefits

When you move into the deep aspects of meditation, your body will engage the parasympathetic nervous system. In this state, your body can digest food, process emotions and thoughts, and send healing modalities wherever they are needed. For many, a simple, daily meditation can provide substantial physical healing. However, such healing is not specific to Tantra; any tradition with meditative practices can provide this.

Unique to Tantra meditation is the purification and revitalization of *nadis* (energy paths in the body—see page 47). Tantra, much like quantum physics, understands energy to be the source of the manifest world. Therefore, when we clean, align, and awaken energy, it harmoniously restructures the physical body. This is especially the case when we bring ayurvedic healing into the Tantra practice.

Within Tantra, many mantras and rituals are explicitly designed to heal the body—both your own and others'. For example, you can take precise action to heal a family member or friend by working with a mantra, yantra, or yajna and the corresponding deity.

Emotional Benefits

Tantra and yoga both hold that the physical influences the emotional and vice versa. That's because when the body is balanced, the emotions are balanced. Through steady Tantrik practice, emotional issues can lessen. Intense emotional outbursts will sublimate as the energy lifts to higher chakras. Self-awareness will build, and you will be able to resolve conflicts with love and compassion. Regular practice can help you feel more empowered, confident, and stabilized in your everyday life.

Mental Benefits

Through persistent sadhana, the tumultuous thoughts that tirelessly push us around dissolve, revealing clarity of mind, discernment, and the ability to listen to Truth.

Tantrik techniques and rituals are pertinent to the purification process of the entire being. Mental purification can take different amounts of time depending on the individual; for some, it can take a very long time. It is only a step within the more extensive process of Awakening, though it may be the most considerable step because our attachment to the mind is often the last to fall away before spiritual achievements.

Spiritual Benefits

For most sadhaks, the primary purpose of Tantra is spiritual benefit. When spiritual attainment is your ultimate goal, blessings within the mental, physical, and emotional realms will also occur.

In Tantra sadhana, the chakras become purified and balanced, awakening Kundalini Shakti. As the practice deepens, the energy flows into the *sushumna nadi* (the central energy channel), rising to the ajna (third eye) chakra and precipitating a focused and luminous mind. Here, you begin to disidentify with your personality.

Once stabilized in the ajna chakra, Kundalini Shakti rises to the crown of the head, where Shiva resides. Here, there is a union of the manifest and the unmanifest, resulting in the last stage of awareness, turiyatita (see page 23). Now you will know yourself as Absolute Awareness. You will be liberated from the impressions of the mind and its will, free to truly be of compassionate service to the betterment of the world.

CHAPTER 3

PRINCIPLES OF TANTRA

There are probably as many types of meditation within Tantra as there are practitioners. In some ways, Tantra is unique because it is flexible and can be easily adapted to meet each practitioner's needs. In this chapter, you will learn about the main principles of Tantrik meditation, as well as the benefits that can be achieved through its practice.

These principles are listed in no particular order. While one principle often supports the unfolding of another, it must be emphasized that Tantra is rarely sequential or determined; all principles and practices are situational, relative, and complementary to one another.

Focusing the Mind

One of the key principles of Tantrik meditation is focus of the mind. Developing focus involves directing the mind to one object. (Remember that for tantrikas, "objects" are both external and internal.) There are countless practices designed to strengthen focus, and the object of concentration varies from tradition to tradition. You may focus on an external object, such as a yantra, a flame, or a physical body sensation, or you may focus on a more internalized object, such as the third eye, a mantra, or passing thoughts.

Focus will come naturally and spontaneously for some. For others, it may require the unblocking of the chakras (see page 38) through a devotional heart or a soft and present body. Focus may also vary based on the psychological, energetic, and karmic disposition of the tantrika. A more heart-oriented disciple may have a more devotional focus, while a more logical disciple may have a more mental focus. Two different disciples may utilize opposing practices within the same tradition; however, no one form of focus is superior to another.

Focus becomes especially important when you seek to perform more advanced sadhanas, and in turn, focus become more refined through such practices.

All of the meditations provided in this book will help you develop focus, stabilize your mind, and improve concentration. With practice, each of the meditations has the potential to guide you to a full, embodied realization.

Breath and Body Awareness

In your daily life, it is easy to become disconnected from your body. This leads many people to wrongly identify with the constellation of thoughts and emotions in the mind, analyzing the past or worrying about the future. By becoming present with the sensations of the body and breath during Tantrik meditation, you can instead come into the present moment.

When you know yourself only as a body, you suffer with the experiences of the body. However, when you observe sensations without trying to control, resist, or hold them, you will come to know yourself as the Absolute Awareness that is the container for the body. In this state, you no longer suffer in your body but witness its sensations as passing clouds.

Many of us know this state as "mindfulness," a term derived from Buddhism. By practicing breath and body awareness, you can turn your attention away from the thoughts and feelings in the mind and towards the experience of sensation within your body. This is done without interpretation, analysis, or judgment.

Breath and body awareness can also help you achieve deep peace and restore the natural equilibrium between your body and mind. This in turn can support focus, help you feel grounded, and assist in awakening the chakras (see page 38). It can even aid you in transcending both the body and mind altogether and knowing yourself as Absolute Awareness.

For some, this awakening can be permanent. For others, it is experienced in fleeting moments. When your identity is rooted in Awareness, you can turn back towards your body and embrace yourself as a divine manifestation within the field of consciousness.

Cultivating Frequencies of Energy

According to Tantra, the Universe was created when Shiva and Shakti were separated. As described earlier, Shiva represents Divine Consciousness, while Shakti represents the energetic force that creates and sustains life. On a universal level, this energy is known simply as Shakti. On an individual, bodily level, it is known as *prana*. It cannot be made or destroyed; it simply changes form.

As Shakti moves throughout our bodies, it regulates all of our bodily functions while also animating and influencing our thoughts and emotions. It flows through a series of channels called nadis, which converge at points called chakras.

Negative occurrences like trauma, accidents, disease, and an unhealthy lifestyle can cause energy to get blocked in the chakras. Tantrik meditation is one technique for unlocking the nadis and activating, circulating, and controlling the flow of energy to unblock and balance the chakras. In this book, we will provide you with a variety of meditations that encourage the circulation of energy, purify the chakras, revitalize the entire energy system, and eventually awaken Kundalini Shakti.

The Seven Chakras

Chakra has become something of a buzzword in modern Western culture. However, due to a lack of accurate translations of Tantrik texts, this wisdom tends to be filtered through Western interpretation and watered down through cultural appropriation, which leads to misinterpretation and confusion. For instance, essential oils, colors, and gemstones supposedly related to chakras have become commonplace and marketable in today's yoga world, but these items were not traditionally related to chakras.

Chakra can be translated literally as "wheel," and like a wheel, chakras have various spokes and a hub in the center. The spokes are the nadis, the energy currents or channels, while the hub is called the *bija*. The chakras are located in the front of the body, and nadis run to the spine, thus connecting the chakras to the spine. A chakra, also called a *padma* (lotus), is depicted by petals surrounding a circle.

A founding Tantrik text, the *Sat Chakra Nirupana*, describes seven chakras. The first five are associated with the five elements of the world (earth, water, fire, air, and space), while the sixth is aligned with the mind and the seventh with Shiva. Each chakra is said to contain special characteristics. With proper training, a practitioner can move energy though them and initiate the ascent of energy. It is very important to note that there are many other lesser-known chakra systems that are also valid yet vary drastically from the seven-chakra system.

Within the seven-chakra system, there exists a dormant energy known as Kundalini Shakti, represented by a sleeping serpent coiled at the base of the spine in the muladhara chakra (see page 41). Tantrik practices such as meditating on the chakras can help balance and harmonize energy. This awakens Kundalini Shakti, which then flows through each chakra. Many people find that even just a slight improvement in the energy system can bring a more peaceful mind, a healthier body, and the ability to manifest a more abundant and vibrant life. When the energy system is fully awakened and Kundalini Shakti has risen to the seventh chakra to unite with Shiva, the tantrika experiences deepened states of awareness and the highest realization.

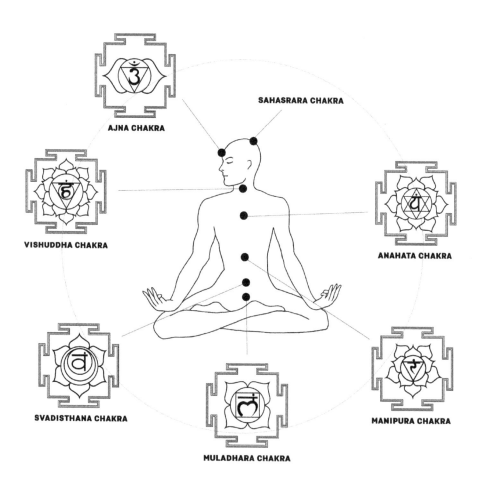

AJNA CHAKRA

SAHASRARA CHAKRA

VISHUDDHA CHAKRA

ANAHATA CHAKRA

SVADISTHANA CHAKRA

MANIPURA CHAKRA

MULADHARA CHAKRA

MULADHARA CHAKRA

ROOT CHAKRA

Location: Perineum

Element: Earth

Earth Element Mantra: *Lam*

Animal: Elephant

Spokes: Four

Ruling Deities: Brahma, Lankini Shakti

Meditative Purpose: To create grounding and a foundation for your spiritual journey

---

NOTE: This is where Kundalini resides.

SVADISTHANA CHAKRA

SACRAL CHAKRA

Location: Sacrum and pubic bone

Element: Water

Water Element Mantra: *Vam*

Animal: Makara (mythical sea creature)

Spokes: Six

Ruling Deities: Rakini, Vishnu

Meditative Purpose: To go beyond our attachment to and identification with sense gratifications

---

NOTE: This is the abode of sexuality and creativity.

MANIPURA CHAKRA

NAVEL CHAKRA

Location: Navel area and the corresponding area in the lumbar spine

Element: Fire

Fire Element Mantra: *Ram*

Animal: Ram (male sheep)

Spokes: 10

Ruling Deities: Rudra Shiva, Lankini Shakti

Meditative Purpose: To awaken the fire of Kundalini and to purify the nadis

---

NOTE: "Manipura" comes from the Sanskrit *mani*, meaning "jewel," and *pura*, meaning "abundance."

ANAHATA CHAKRA

HEART CHAKRA

Location: Center of the chest and the corresponding region in the thoracic spine

Element: Air

Air Element Mantra: *Yam*

Animal: Antelope

Spokes: 12

Ruling Deity: Ishvara

Meditative Purpose: To begin the process of letting go of personal desires and worldly attachments

---

NOTE: The Linga (an icon of Shiva) is symbolized as being in the center of anahata. This indicates the potential to enter into Supreme Shiva Consciousness through anahata.

VISHUDDHA CHAKRA

THROAT CHAKRA

Location: Center of the throat and the corresponding region in the cervical spine

Element: *Akasha* (ether or space)

Space Element Mantra: *Ham*

Animal: White elephant

Spokes: 16

Ruling Deities: Panchavaktra Shiva, Shakti Shankini

Meditative Purpose: To move from the immanent towards the transcendent

---

NOTE: "Vishuddha" means "pure" and is expressed through a purity of life. However, the inability to express oneself does not mean vishuddha is blocked.

AJNA CHAKRA

THIRD EYE CHAKRA

Location: Center of the forehead

Element: None

Mantra: *Aum*

Animal: None

Spokes: Two

Ruling Deities: Ardhanarishvara (Shiva manifested as half woman and half man), Hakini Shakti

Meditative Purpose: To have control over the mind

NOTE: "Ajna" means "command," so the ajna chakra is sometimes referred to as the mental command center. With the ajna chakra, we are moving beyond the material realm, so there is no element associated with this chakra.

SAHASRARA CHAKRA

CROWN CHAKRA

Location: Crown of the head

Element: None

Mantra: None

Animal: None

Spokes: 1,000

Ruling Deity: Paramashiva

Meditative Purpose: Ultimate transcendence into the formless state

---

NOTE: Often not really considered a chakra because it is beyond all form, sahasrara is symbolic of the transcendental. It is beyond all space and time and therefore has no associated symbol or element.

Nadis

The Sanskrit text the *Shiva Samhita* states that there are more than 300,000 nadis in the human body. Tantra focuses on three main nadis. Two run down either side of the spine; they are called *ida* and *pingala*. The ida nadi runs along the left side of the spine and accounts for feelings of stupor, lethargy, and laziness. The pingala nadi runs along the right side of the spine and accounts for feelings of restlessness, overexcitement, and agitation.

The third nadi runs through the middle of the spine and is called the sushumna nadi (the central channel). When the energy of the ida and pingala nadis are balanced, the energy of the practitioner spontaneously moves into the sushumna nadi. This activates Kundalini Shakti, which moves through each chakra on her way up the spine until she unites with Shiva in the sahasrara chakra.

Awakening the Hridaya (Heart)

For the tantrika, the *hridaya* (heart) is especially sacred. The hridaya is neither the physical heart nor the anahata chakra; it is the deepest Consciousness, the heart of Shiva and the source of Shakti. From the hridaya, Shakti blossoms outwards, manifesting the world, only to dissolve back into the vastness of Shiva's heart. The hridaya is the location-less temple in which Shiva and Shakti perform their eternal cosmic dance.

When you learn to keep your citta (individual Consciousness) focused on hridaya, you will no longer identify with the body-mind and you will dissolve into turiya (see page 21) and eventually turi-yatita (see page 23).

Through this practice alone, you can come to self-realization. If you can withdraw the senses from the external world and focus on the hridaya, this will be the only method needed, and you can discard all other rigorous practices.

However, this level of absorption is not possible without absolute focus. The mind will try to distract you, but you must witness whatever desires and distractions arise with honest acceptance and nonjudgment. As these attributes are cultivated internally, you will replicate them in the external world. Meeting the difficulties and desires of your mind with deep acceptance and nonjudgment, you will come to meet the supposed "other" with the same compassion. There are many meditations in chapter 7 that can be utilized to establish and deepen one's connection with the hridaya.

Realizing Tantrik Non-Duality

In Hinduism, there are two perspectives on the relationship between the Divine and the individual soul:

- **Dualism:** Also known as *dvaita*, this perspective posits that the Divine is distinct from the jiva.
- **Non-dualism:** Also known as *advaita*, this perspective holds that the Divine and the jiva are indivisible.

The fundamentals of non-dual philosophy spring from the sacred texts of the Vedas. Vedanta, an Indian philosophy based around the Vedas, is one of the most popular philosophies in yogic circles. Vedanta states that everything in the manifest world is an illusion, something to be transcended. Practitioners of Vedanta often deny the manifest and refrain from involving themselves in the world. Tantra, in contrast, understands that everything is divine and therefore that the manifest is as real and as important as the transcendent.

The path is unique for each practitioner and may serve them in a variety of ways depending on where they are in their spiritual journey. Each philosophy is like a different finger pointing to the same moon. Vedanta and dualistic Tantra can give us the perspective required to realize our Divinity. Non-dual Tantra can give us the ability to embody this understanding in our everyday lives.

Regardless of the path taken, the non-dualistic understanding will not be fully realized until the manifest and the unmanifest are embraced as one and the same. Tantra believes that as long as we deny the world, we resist the Divine in the manifest. In this denial, we create separation, and in separation, we suffer. In chapter 8, you will be presented with meditations that can help you experience and realize the non-dual.

PART 2

TANTRIK MEDITATION

The following meditation practices are robust and an excellent way to begin or expand upon your meditative practice. Each is based on a traditional practice or has been adapted to create a modern practice. (We've noted which practices are adapted.) Remember that learning directly from an empowered teacher is the traditional approach to Tantra and will bring you the greatest benefits from these meditations.

The methods in this section are diverse. There is no specific order in which these meditations must be done. In Tantra, the categories of meditation are not necessarily sequential, though sometimes one meditation can be a prerequisite for another. We recommend you start with the meditations to which you are intuitively drawn.

Each meditation includes a suggested amount of time for which to practice it. It can help to set a timer so that you don't have to actively keep track of how much time has passed during your meditations.

For many, enlightenment can only be achieved with the guidance and wisdom of an authentic guru. However, this book can still bring extraordinary shifts in consciousness and an awakening of Kundalini, even if you have no formal experience in meditation. Whether or not this happens to you will depend on numerous factors, including but not limited to your dedication, consistency, karma, and astrology.

TIPS FOR MEDITATION

If you are new to meditation, the following tips will help you get started. As with any skill, the more you practice meditation, more naturally it will come to you.

- **Find a suitable setting:** Create a quiet meditation spot in your home where you feel comfortable and will not be disturbed.

- **Find the right posture:** For some meditations, it is key to make sure that your body is completely relaxed. You can support your back with a pillow or other cushion if there is any strain. At other times, it is crucial that you hold your body in a cross-legged position on the ground so that you are in direct contact with the earth. This contact helps bring stability to the body and mind. When the spine is in an upright position, the spinal column's energy and chakras will flow appropriately. Each meditation will include sitting instructions.

- **Breathe naturally:** Some of the meditations may ask you to breathe in a particular manner. If no specific instructions are given, simply allow the breath to be soft, natural, and comfortable—whatever is easiest for you.

- **Allow thoughts to pass:** Some days, it can feel challenging to meditate, especially if you are feeling tired or restless. If this is the case, try to allow thoughts to naturally come and go, rather than engaging with them and being pushed off course by the winds of the mind.

- **Create a daily practice:** It can help to put aside a set time each day to meditate in order to make it a daily practice. This might be after you wake up or before you go to sleep.

CHAPTER 4

MEDITATIONS FOR FOCUSING THE MIND

Mental focus is an essential aspect of Tantra and other meditative spiritual disciplines. Without focus, Tantrik techniques will yield minimal outcomes. At the same time, Tantra is unique because the practice of ritual and the various Tantrik tools allow a beginner tantrika to move through multiple methods and sadhana without necessarily having good focus.

Regardless, at some point in sadhana, all practitioners will have to bring control over the mind. Once the mind is focused, the practitioner becomes absorbed into the object of concentration, and meditation begins. This starts the deepening into the various stages of awareness, to the point of turiya and even turiyatita.

Focusing on a Flame

TIME: 20 MINUTES · TYPE: TRADITIONAL

The practice of gazing at a candle flame comes from the *Hatha Yoga Pradipika*. This particular style of focus meditation is called "Trataka" and can be done with almost any object, but the flame is the traditional choice. This practice brings focus to the mind and helps awaken the energy in the ajna (third eye) chakra (see page 46).

1. Put a candle or oil lamp at an arm's length in front of you. Place it at eye level so that you are not putting any undue pressure on your neck to look at it. Light the candle or lamp.

2. Find a comfortable seated position, with your spine straight and erect but relaxed. The preferred position is cross-legged on the floor, as it aids the mind's focus. However, this meditation can also be done while sitting in a chair.

3. Keeping your spine straight and erect, soften the rest of your body and begin gazing at the flame. Bring your attention to the middle of your forehead while gazing. Try to imagine that you are looking at the flame from the middle of your forehead.

4. Focus solely on the flame and allow the mind to empty of all thought. If thoughts come, let them pass by without getting caught up in them. Let this be effortless, with a restful feeling in the body.

5. At some point, your eyes may feel like they want to close. Allow this to happen but continue to focus on the flame in your mind's eye.

6. After 20 minutes of gazing, rub your hands together gently, warming the palms. Place them over your eyes to bring healing energy to the eyes.

7. Give yourself a moment to be present with sensations in your forehead area. Notice the activation of the ajna chakra, the increased sensitivity in the middle of your forehead, and the focus of the mind.

TIP: This practice can be performed with a soft gaze or an unblinking gaze.

Visualizing an OM Symbol

TIME: 15 MINUTES · TYPE: TRADITIONAL/MODERN

The visualization of an OM symbol is a fantastic practice for focus. Often, our imaginations work against us, pulling us into creative worlds and dreams and distracting us from meditation. However, in this practice, you will use the mind's creativity to help bring focus. This practice will also help purify your mind and bring peace into your entire being.

1. Draw or print a large OM symbol on an 8″ x 11″ piece of paper. It is preferable to make the OM symbol golden, as this color relates to the ajna (third eye) chakra.

2. Place the image on a wall at eye level. A white or pale-colored wall is best; if all your walls are dark, find a blank wall with few distracting objects on it. Ensure that the room is well-lit.

3. Find a comfortable, seated position. A cross-legged position on the floor is helpful, but this meditation can also be done in a chair.

4. Allow your eyes to gaze softly at the OM symbol in front of you. Try to gaze at the image without blinking.

5. After a minute, slowly and gently close your eyes. Focus on the image of the OM symbol as it appears on your eyelids, behind closed eyes.

6. Hold on to the image for as long as you can. Dwell on the image and attempt to make it clear and sharp in your mind's eye. When the image is lost, slowly open your eyes and begin gazing at the OM symbol again.

7. If you cannot see the OM symbol's image in your mind's eye or if thoughts come to you, do not be frustrated. Be patient and open your eyes again, repeating steps 4 through 6.

8. After 15 minutes, allow yourself to notice the radiant vibration of the ajna chakra in the middle of your forehead. The mind is clear and sharp.

TIP: You can also put the OM symbol in the light of a candle or a lightbulb to make it glow. The glow helps imprint the image of the OM symbol behind closed eyes. This can make the visualization easier in the beginning.

Meditating on the Third Eye

TIME: 10 MINUTES · TYPE: MODERN

This simple yet powerful practice requires internal, rather than external, focus. While summoning this focus can be challenging for some, it is an important ability to develop in Tantrik meditation. During this meditation, you will concentrate on your third eye, an energetic inner eye located in the center of the forehead. This can improve focus by activating the ajna (third eye) chakra. The hatha yoga text the *Gheranda Samhita* states that this meditation can promote clairvoyance. It can also improve memory.

1. Sit in a comfortable position, with a straight and erect spine. Allow the rest of your body to be relaxed and soft.

2. Close your eyes and focus your mind on the third eye in the middle of your forehead.

3. If thoughts come, allow them but do not be disturbed by them. Know that if you do not engage with them, they will go as quickly as they came. Simply stay focused on the third eye.

4. At some point in this meditation, a point of light may appear behind your closed eyes. Allow your focus to rest on this point.

5. Let your attention be absorbed into the third eye and your mind deepen in meditation.

6. After 10 minutes, take a moment to be aware of an increased focus, increased concentration on one point, and increased energy in the third eye.

TIP: Placing a drop of peppermint oil in the middle of your forehead can help you stay focused on the third eye.

Yantra-Drawing Meditation

TIME: 15 TO 20 MINUTES · TYPE: MODERN

In Tantra, during the ritualistic process of building a yantra, one of the key steps is the drawing of the yantra. Creating the shapes required to give the yantra form attunes the practitioner to the subtle energies symbolized by the yantra. In this practice, you will draw or paint one of the yantras of the chakras that are shown in the chakra section of chapter 3 (see pages 40 to 46). Gather a sheet of paper and some pencils, pens, or paints to draw with. Many find it easier to focus when there is a cultivation of love and devotion, and this is a wonderful practice for that cultivation.

1. Decide which yantra you will draw or paint from the chakra yantra diagrams in chapter 3. Try to choose a chakra with qualities that you feel are lacking in your life.

2. Find a quiet and peaceful space where you will be undisturbed.

3. Light a candle and place it at arm's length in front of you. Take a moment to connect with your heart and to acknowledge that you will be honoring the Divine in its sacred geometric form. Do this for one minute.

4. Close your eyes and perceive the form of the yantra. Do your best to visualize the yantra behind closed eyes. Feel a sense of reverence and devotion for this divine form. Do this for two minutes.

5. Begin to draw or paint your chosen yantra. Take your time. If you notice that your mind is wandering and not mindful of the task at hand, bring your attention back to the yantra. Continue to cultivate an adoration and humility for the opportunity to bring the Divine into form.

6. When you're finished, take a moment with your eyes closed to feel the energy of your chosen chakra activate in your body. Do this for one to two minutes.

TIP: You may need other tools to aid in drawing your chosen yantra, such as a ruler and compass. For some people, this meditation may take longer than 20 minutes; you are welcome to come back to it the next day.

Yantra-Gazing Meditation

TIME: 5 TO 20 MINUTES · TYPE: MODERN

In the world of Tantra, we can manifest the subtle effects of the energetic body of an object by simply focusing our attention upon it. A yantra is a sacred and divine object with a potent and powerful energetic body. It is due to this potency that when we focus on a yantra, manifesting its qualities within ourselves is easier. In this meditation, you will use the yantras contained in the chakra section of chapter 3 of this book or the yantra you created in the "Yantra-Drawing Meditation" (see page 62) to awaken specific energies within yourself.

1. Find a chakra from chapter 3 that you would like to work with. Try to choose one that calls to you and has qualities you would like to manifest.

2. Find a comfortable position either cross-legged on the floor or sitting in a chair.

3. Turn to the page of this book that contains the chakra and corresponding yantra you would like to work with. Prop the book up in front of you, preferably at forehead height. If this is not possible, then place it on your lap or on the floor in front of you.

4. Take one minute with your eyes closed to perceive the yantra in front of you. Try to feel the subtle qualities of the yantra radiating from the page.

5. Open your eyes and bring them to gaze upon the center of your chosen chakra-yantra. Allow this gaze to be soft, with eyes half closed.

6. At points, the eyes may want to wander. Gently bring them back to the center of the yantra.

7. The mind will also wander. In the same way, bring your focus back to the yantra.

8. After 15 minutes, close your eyes and see if you can visualize the yantra behind your eyelids. If you can, keep your focus pointed internally at the yantra until it dissipates.

9. At the end of your meditation, bring your attention to the place where your chosen chakra is located in your body and feel its shining vibrancy and activation.

TIP: If your eyes get tired or begin to water, take a moment to close them. Rub your hands together quickly until warmth is generated, then bring them over your eyes and feel soothing energy radiate from your palms.

Closing the Gates of Sensation

TIME: 5 TO 10 MINUTES · TYPE: TRADITIONAL

This practice is traditionally called "Sanmukhi Mudra," which can be translated as the "Six-Gated Mudra." It involves redirecting awareness internally by closing the six gates of outer perception: the two ears, the two eyes, the nose, and the mouth. This is an intense practice that brings a strong pranic force towards the third eye. It helps the practitioner unlock the energies there, transcend the mind, and rest as the witness.

1. Sit in a comfortable position on the floor or in a chair. Make sure that your spine is straight and erect.

2. Exhale all of the air in your lungs. Then, fill your lungs with a large inhalation and hold your breath for as long as you can without straining. (You will exhale again in step 4.) Bring your hands to your face and close your head's six openings with your fingers. Place your thumbs in your ears, your index fingers on your eyes, your middle fingers on your nostrils, your ring fingers on your upper lip, and your pinkies on your lower lip. Now the six gates are closed.

3. Continue to hold your breath for as long as you can. You may notice a light behind your closed eyes. Focus your attention there.

4. When your body has the natural urge to exhale, exhale. Do not hold your breath any longer. After you have exhaled, allow your breath to return to a natural, calm, and steady state.

5. Gently fall into a silent meditation practice and rest in the silent stillness that this mudra brings.

TIP: When first performing this practice, you should only hold your breath for as long as it is comfortable. If a pinpoint of light does not appear in the middle of your forehead, that is fine; it is not that important. Gradually work up to holding your breath for longer periods of time, performing multiple rounds of this practice over 5 to 10 minutes total.

Noticing the Gaps

TYPE: TRADITIONAL

This unconventional practice can be incorporated into your evening sleep routine. It is drawn from the *Vijnana Bhairava Tantra*, a Tantrik text that says there is a gap of emptiness between any two states of awareness. This meditation aims to find the silent gap between waking and sleeping. This is the silence of turiyatita (see page 23), the sacred space between all states of awareness through which we can realize the Self spontaneously.

1. Lie down in whatever position you usually fall asleep in. Close your eyes and allow your body to become soft and relaxed.

2. Allow your mind and thoughts to slow, gently bringing your awareness to the point where the mind begins to move from waking (jagrat) into dreaming (svapna).

3. Your awareness of the outer world will begin to fade, and the inner world's silence will emerge. Your awareness will feel as though it is suspended between jagrat and svapna. Stay attentive to this suspended state; it is the silence of turiyatita, the sacred space between all states of awareness.

4. Resting in silent awareness, you may notice dreams or thoughts begin to play in your mind. Remain aware and do not be distracted by them. Treat them in the same way that you treat thoughts in any other meditation: Notice them, but do not identify or engage with them. Know that they will come and go.

5. Stay in this state for as long as you can, until you fall asleep. A master of Tantra will never go unconscious and will remain in turiyatita throughout the entire night.

TIP: This meditation can be resumed and practiced in the morning as you move from dreaming to waking. Notice again your awareness suspended between the two states, and simply be.

Bhairava Meditation

TIME: 20 MINUTES · TYPE: MODERN

In Tantra, Bhairava is the most fierce and frightening form of Shiva. Shiva is the great emptiness, and Bhairava is the terrifying and exquisite experience we can have in contemplating that emptiness. On the one hand, this leads you to face the unknown, which can often mean confronting the notion of death. On the other hand, it ultimately brings great freedom as all effort, holding, grasping, or striving that you carry in everyday life dissolves into the unknown.

1. Sit in a comfortable position, preferably cross-legged on the floor. You can use a chair if necessary.

2. Bring your eyes to gaze upon an empty space on the floor, about six feet in front of you. Your eyes should feel like they are resting naturally, without effort. Do not look at anything in particular. Allow your gaze to be soft and unfocused.

3. Rest as the witness. If you do not identify with any thoughts, sensations, or emotions that arise, you will experience a vast, limitless emptiness.

4. Transcending both body and mind, gently try to find the source of your being within this vast, empty space. Keep your eyes open.

5. If you are gripped by fear, remember that meditation cannot harm you. If necessary, return to the relaxing sensation of the breath running in and out of the body.

6. At the end of the meditation, take a moment to savor the sweet and gentle quiet of the mind.

TIP: Be patient with this practice, as even a momentary state of emptiness can be remarkably beneficial.

The OM Mantra

TIME: 20 MINUTES · TYPE: TRADITIONAL

The three sounds of the OM mantra (spelled phonetically as "AUM") each represent one of the initial states of awareness: waking, dreaming, and sleeping. By chanting "AUM" and focusing on each of these sounds separately, the three states merge, and in the silence that follows, you may be able to experience the transcendental state of turiya (see page 21).

1. Sit in a comfortable, cross-legged position in which your spine is straight and there is space for your belly to expand on a full inhalation. If you find that this position restricts your belly from expanding because your thighs are off the ground, try sitting in a kneeling position or in a chair instead.

2. Take a big inhalation. Then, breath out slowly as you chant the three sounds of the OM mantra. Remember that the entire word is chanted in one fluid exhalation.

   a. Chant the "A" with your mouth wide open to make an "aw" sound.
   b. Close your mouth slightly for the "U" to make an "ew" sound.
   c. Close your lips to hum the "M" sound.

3. Take a moment to rest briefly in silence, then repeat the mantra.

4. As you repeat the mantra, imagine energy moving through your body: from your chest when you chant "A," to your throat during "U," to your third eye during "M," and out of the top of your head during the silence that follows.

5. After chanting this mantra repeatedly for 15 minutes, stop and rest in silence for five minutes. Notice the purity of your mind and the bath of peace washing over your body. With consistent practice, this meditation may lead to the transcendental state of turiya.

TIP: This practice can also be performed by repeating the mantra inwardly (see "Inner OM Mantra" on page 120). This can challenge you to maintain focus without being able to concentrate on the vibrations of outward chanting.

Focus on the Heart Center

TIME: 20 MINUTES · TYPE: TRADITIONAL

This practice helps you become completely absorbed in the hridaya (heart). When you are absorbed in the hridaya, you not only know but also *are* complete and lasting peace and contentment. Although the focus of this meditation is in the center of the chest, this location is only symbolic. The hridaya is actually without location and is known as the heart of Shiva. In some Tantrik circles, the hridaya is referred to as the "spiritual heart," but it should not be confused with anahata.

1. Sit or lie down in any comfortable position.

2. Close your eyes or softly gaze at nothing in particular. Allow your body to become relaxed. Take a moment to settle your mind and body.

3. Bring your attention to the space in the middle of your chest. It can be helpful to place a hand over your heart or to notice how your breath runs over this area with each inhalation and exhalation.

4. Thoughts, sensations, and tricks of the mind will come to distract you. Stay attentive to the sacred space in the middle of your chest. Slowly, a natural state of *pratyahara* (a withdrawal of the senses) will come over your being. Allow your awareness to withdraw from external distractions and become wholly absorbed into this space.

5. Notice if Absolute Awareness begins to come to the forefront of your attention.

6. When time is up, take a moment to feel a sense of gratitude and the presence of being.

TIP: This practice can be done in any position at any time. It is good to have a formal daily time set aside for it, but it can also be performed while waiting in line, while sitting on a bus, before eating a meal, or even before going to sleep.

CHAPTER 5

MEDITATIONS FOR BREATH AND BODY AWARENESS

Unlike other spiritual traditions, Tantra does not perceive the body as an illusion, an obstacle, or a sin. Instead, Tantra perceives the body and all that is manifested as a vibrant constellation of the Divine expressed in form. Some Tantrik breath and body practices are designed to prepare us for spiritual development and realization. Others are concluding practices that help us complete our full embodied realization. In some ways, the breath and body are both the start and the end of the Tantrik journey.

  Continuously returning to the practices in this chapter will only strengthen your discipline, deepen your understanding, and expand your being.

Alternate-Nostril Breathing

TIME: 5 TO 10 MINUTES · TYPE: MODERN

In Tantra and Hatha Yoga (which came from Tantra), the human energy system is directly associated with the breath. When breathing is calm, energy is calm; when breathing is chaotic, the mind is cluttered. As noted in the section of this book on nadis (see page 47), human energy moves between the left and the right nadi constantly, bringing either a passive type of energy or an active one. This breathing meditation helps balance both energies into the central channel, bringing a state of meditation naturally, as the body's energy is in balance and flowing when in the central channel (sushumna nadi).

1. Find a comfortable seated position, either on the floor or in a chair. Make sure your back is straight and vertical.

2. With your eyes closed, inhale and exhale deeply three times through your nose.

3. With your right hand, bring your thumb to rest beside your right nostril, and your ring finger next to your left nostril. Place your middle finger in the third eye area in the middle of your forehead.

4. Close your right nostril with your thumb and inhale through your left nostril. Hold the breath in for as long as is comfortable.

5. Close your left nostril with your ring finger and exhale through your right nostril. Hold the breath out for as long as is comfortable.

6. Keeping your left nostril closed, inhale through your right nostril. Hold your breath in for as long as is comfortable.

7. Close your right nostril and exhale through your left nostril. Hold your breath out for as long as is comfortable.

8. Steps 3 through 7 are one round. Continue for 3 to 10 rounds.

9. When you're finished, take a moment to feel an inner calmness and harmony, a natural feeling of wanting to continue to meditate.

TIP: Sometimes at the beginning of such a practice, you may feel lightheaded, so it's good to take this practice gently and with care. However, if the feeling persists or if you feel like you might faint, discontinue this practice.

Earthly Senses

TIME: 20 MINUTES · TYPE: MODERN

In many traditions, the "material world" is seen as something that must be transcended and overcome. In Tantra, we use these very "obstacles" as an opportunity. Tantrikas understand that everything is Divine, so everything can be used as a tool to discover the Divine. In this meditation, you will use your senses to become deeply intimate with the material world, until you come to a place of union with that which you perceive.

This meditation is best practiced in a place where you can be surrounded by wild and untamed nature and where you cannot see people or evidence of people, such as houses, fences, or powerlines. However, if nature is inaccessible, it can also be practiced in the city. Do your best to remove as many "unnatural" objects from view as possible.

This meditation can be practiced sitting, standing, or walking. However, if you are walking, it should be without direction, without following a path or having a specific place you want to end up, intuitive and aimless.

1. Sitting, standing, or walking, become aware of your body. Become aware of your breath flowing in and out of your lungs. Become aware of the sensations of your body and where it makes contact with the earth. Notice where the air that surrounds you touches your skin. Feel the wind in your hair. If you like, you can take off your shoes and feel the ground beneath your feet. Take a moment to touch your hand to a tree or a nearby plant. Be fully present with your sense of feeling in this natural space.

2. Bring your attention now to your sense of sight. Become aware of the variety of colors that surround you. Notice the way that the light illuminates different areas in this natural setting. Become mindful of the variety of shapes and sizes of forms that surround you. Open your eyes to the details of this natural setting. If you're walking, be sure to go slow and take in the details, such as the bark of a tree, the earth beneath your feet, or the leaves on the branches. Be fully present with your sense of sight.

3. Now, wherever you are, become aware of your sense of hearing. It may be easier for you to do this if you close your eyes. Become aware of the sounds that are closest to your body. Become aware of the sounds that are loudest and easiest to hear. Notice the subtler sounds surrounding you, as well as sounds off in the distance—the sound of the wind, the sound of your breath. Be fully present with your sense of hearing.

>>

4. Become aware of your sense of smell. Bring your nose close to flowers, the bark of a tree, and the earth's moss or grass. Freely indulge your sense of smell in this natural and wild place.

5. Become aware of your senses simultaneously: the sound of the wind, the smell of the earth, the sight of nature, and the feeling of your body touching the ground.

6. Take a big breath in and out. Feel gratitude for the sacred space around you and all of the gifts it has to offer. Recognize and appreciate the beauty of this moment and the peace that it brings you in being fully present.

TIP: This meditation can also be done while focusing on only one sense, such as focusing on just the sense of sound.

Shaking Meditation

TIME: 5 TO IO MINUTES · TYPE: MODERN

Being present in the body and using sensation as a focal point in meditation is a unique part of Tantra. However, sometimes you can feel overwhelmed and even consumed by your mind and the tension that it creates in your body. This can make your body feel like an inhospitable place to be. This meditation is a simple practice for releasing stagnant or pent-up energy and bringing your body back into a place of balance.

1. Come to a standing position with your feet about hip-width apart. Plant your feet firmly on the ground, with a small bend in your knees, and spread your toes wide. Let your shoulders be soft and relaxed. Soften the muscles around your eyes and jaw. Take a few deep breaths in and out. Soften your gaze or close your eyes.

2. Keeping your feet rooted to the ground, shake your body gently and quickly. Shake every part of your body and pay particular attention to those areas that are resisting the meditation and remaining still. While you do this, take some big breaths in and out through the nose and sigh loudly. Shake like this for 5 to 10 minutes.

3. When you're ready, come back to a still, strong standing position. Keep your eyes closed, or keep a soft gaze, looking at nothing in particular. Become aware of your senses: the sensation of your body, the energy running through your system, your breath, and the sound of silence around you. Spend a few minutes simply noticing your present state of being.

4. Take a few more full, long, slow breaths and bring your practice to a close. Feel gratitude for the ability to reset and release.

TIP: Many will find this practice easier to do when alone. It can be challenging to let go and thoroughly shake without feeling self-conscious when others are nearby.

Body Awareness

TIME: 10 MINUTES · TYPE: MODERN

Tantra teaches us that when the body is at peace, the mind will often follow. However, many people identify so deeply with their minds that they are completely disassociated from their bodies. This practice will help you find an embodied sense of presence and tranquility.

1. This meditation is best practiced lying down. With your eyes open or closed, take a few big breaths and settle into position.

2. As you bring your attention to the different parts of your body, let it rest on each spot for three seconds, or a few breaths, before moving on.

3. Bring awareness to your left leg and mentally scan each part of it. Notice any sensation in the toes, bottom of the foot, top of the foot, lower leg, knee, upper thigh, glute, hip, and pelvis.

4. Bring awareness to your right leg and scan each part of it.

5. Bring awareness to your left arm and scan each part of it. Notice any sensation in the fingers, palm of the hand, back of the hand, wrist, lower arm, elbow, upper arm, underarm, and shoulder.

6. Bring awareness to your right arm and scan each part of it.

7. Bring awareness to the front of your torso and scan each part of it. Notice any sensation in the lower belly, belly button, upper belly, front of the ribs, chest, collarbones, and front of the neck.

8. Bring awareness to the back of your torso and scan each part of it. Notice any sensation in the lower back, middle back, back of the ribs, shoulder blades, back of the neck, base of the spine, middle of the spine, upper spine, vertebrae in the neck, and base of the skull.

9. Bring awareness to your face and scan each part of it. Notice any sensation in the jaw, cheeks, chin, lips, mouth, cheekbones, nose, eyes, eyebrows, temples, forehead, ears, sides of the head, and top of the head.

10. Be aware of your whole body. Take three big breaths and slowly bring movement into your fingers and toes. Roll onto one side. Take a few more breaths and, when you're ready, return to a seated posture.

11. Take a moment to feel the peacefulness cultivated within your body and mind.

TIP: This practice can also be done while sitting in a chair, sitting on the ground, or standing. The point is to find a position where you can really relax your body.

Rocking Meditation

TIME: 20 MINUTES · TYPE: TRADITIONAL

Tantrikas believe that while a still body can bring the mind to silence, the mind can also be still while the body is in motion (such as in traditional forms of Indian dance). Although there is a connection between mind and body, it is not always direct. In this meditation, inspired by the *Vijnana Bhairava Tantra*, you will swing or rock your body while meditating. This practice explores how the mind can be brought into a profound stillness even when there is movement of the body.

1. Find a comfortable seated posture, making sure that your back is not resting against anything. The upper part of your body should be free to move and sway.

2. Close your eyes and bring your awareness to the middle of your chest. Focus on the breath flowing in and out.

3. Slowly begin to allow your body to sway without moving your arms. This could start with a very gentle movement from one side to the other. Let your body move by itself, slowly, without consciously controlling its movements. Allow it to be spontaneous with small gestures.

4. If your body wants to rotate, allow it to. If it wants to move forward and backward, allow it to. Let yourself flow into the swaying movement. Again, don't move to any rhythm or inner music. Just sway.

5. Notice your mind coming more and more into a feeling of centeredness and emptiness.

6. Continue for 15 minutes.

7. Finally, come to a place of stillness. Rest in the witnessing awareness of emptiness.

TIP: This practice can also be done while standing. In standing practice, try not to bring a dancing type of movement to your body. Instead, allow your body to sway back and forth effortlessly and spontaneously.

Taste Meditation

TIME: 20 MINUTES · TYPE: MODERN

Tantra posits that all manifestations in this Universe can be utilized to deepen the state of awareness and eventually move into the non-dual. That's why using the senses for focus and deepening awareness is a typical Tantrik practice.

This practice is ideal for any time you are sitting (preferably alone) in a quiet place. Using the sensation of taste, you will touch upon pleasant feelings, which have their root in blissfulness. By following pleasurable sensations into blissfulness, you can become blissful. By expanding on these sensations, you can let go of specific phenomena and enter the great blissfulness of Self-Awareness.

1. Make yourself a warm beverage. It should be something that is soothing for you, such as tea or hot chocolate. Try to stay away from overstimulating beverages like coffee.

2. Find a comfortable position in a chair or even on a sofa.

3. Hold the cup in your hands, feeling its warmth. Then, close your eyes, being careful not to spill your drink.

4. Bring your attention to your heart space. Focus on your breath in the center of your chest. Feel it come into your body, and feel it leave your body. Do this for a few minutes, becoming more and more centered.

5. When you feel that you have calmed down your mind and your body, begin to notice the subtleties of your sensations, like the feeling of the cup in your hands, the smell of your beverage, or the pleasant feeling of relaxation in your body.

6. Next, slowly move the cup to your lips, being mindful of your movements, and take a sip of your beverage. Do not swallow.

7. Notice the warmth and the taste of the liquid and how it brings a feeling of enjoyment. Slowly swallow the liquid, holding on to the joyful sensations.

8. Allow this joyful feeling to overwhelm your entire body, energy, and mind until everything is united in Absolute Bliss.

9. When you notice your mind starting its chatter again or a feeling of an individualized self returning, repeat steps 6 through 8. Continue until the beverage is finished, or about 15 minutes have passed.

10. Finally, take a moment to be aware of your profound journey to the Absolute and back again through the agency of pleasant sensations. Spend a few minutes being grateful to your loved ones to close the meditation.

TIP: You might find it helpful to do either the "Body Awareness" practice (see page 86) or "Alternate-Nostril Breathing" practice (see page 78) before this one.

Silent Breath

TIME: 20 MINUTES · TYPE: MODERN

In meditation, when you begin to go deep into a practice, the body becomes still and the breath becomes light and almost imperceptible. This meditation is a preliminary practice to help one go deeper in the stages of meditation by slowing the breath and bringing calmness into the body and mind. It is great for both beginners and more advanced practitioners (as a way to prepare for other meditations in this book).

1. Sit in a comfortable posture with a straight, relaxed spine. Cross-legged is best, but you can sit in a chair if you prefer.

2. With your eyes open or closed, bring your awareness to your body, and mentally scan it from your toes to the top of your head. If you feel tension in any part of your body, allow your breath to caress and dissipate it. Spend a few minutes here.

3. Bring your awareness to the center of your chest. Perceive how your breath causes the rising and falling of the chest area.

4. As the meditation continues, allow your breath to slow down and become subtler and subtler. You'll notice that as you deepen in Awareness, your breath will feel almost like it has stopped.

5. Remain in this space of calmness for as long as you can.

6. After 20 minutes, slowly come back to normal breathing and open your eyes if you closed them. Take a moment to rest in the calming awareness that this meditation brings.

TIP: In this meditation, do not hold your breath so that you feel like you're gasping for air. Instead, let this process of slowing down your breath feel as natural as possible.

Yoga Nidra

TIME: 20 MINUTES · TYPE: TRADITIONAL

This is a traditional form of meditation that has been adapted over generations. It was first described in the *Mandukya Upanishad* and is referenced in the story of Vishnu floating upon the primordial waters. This meditation can help tantrikas release tension from the body, calm the nervous system, overcome fears, release attachment to the body, and come to full Self-Realization. It can be done on its own or as a preliminary meditation before a more advanced practice.

1. Lie on the ground flat on your back. It can be helpful to place pillows under your knees and behind your head. Allow your body to release any final movements before coming into a place of deep rest and stillness.

2. Closing your eyes, or with a soft gaze, bring your attention to your breath. Start to extend and lengthen your inhalations and exhalations. Feel, visualize, or witness the breath coming in through the bottoms of your feet and traveling up to your heart.

3. Hold your breath for a moment in your heart. Notice the silence and stillness permeating from your heart. Exhale and feel the breath flow out of the top of your head into the ether beyond. Repeat.

4. Slowly release the visualization and allow the breath to return to a gentle, uncontrolled, natural rhythm.

5. Slowly move your attention through the following 61 points.

6. Rest in complete stillness. Witness the body breathing naturally as it lies on the floor.

>>

Continued

1. Middle of the forehead
2. Center of the throat
3. Right shoulder joint
4. Right elbow joint
5. Middle of the right wrist
6. Tip of the right thumb
7. Tip of the index finger
8. Tip of the middle finger
9. Tip of the fourth finger (ring finger)
10. Tip of the small finger
11. Right wrist joint
12. Right elbow joint
13. Right shoulder joint
14. Center of the throat

15–26. Repeat points 3 to 14 on the left side.

27. The heart center
28. Right nipple
29. The heart center
30. Left nipple
31. The heart center
32. Navel
33. Pubis
34. Right hip joint
35. Right knee joint
36. Right ankle joint
37. The right big toe
38. Tip of the second toe
39. Tip of the third toe
40. Tip of the fourth toe
41. Tip of the small toe
42. Right ankle joint
43. Right knee joint
44. Right hip joint
45. Pubis

46–56. Repeat points 34 to 44 on the left side.

57. Pubis
58. Navel
59. The heart center
60. Center of the throat
61. Middle of the forehead

7. Slowly bring movement into your fingers and toes. Allow your arms to reach up overhead for a big stretch. Roll onto one side and take a few breaths. Come up into a seated posture and bring your hands over the heart center. Take a moment to feel the peace, tranquility, and overall presence radiating within.

TIP: We recommend that you take some time to run through the 61 points included in this meditation before beginning it so that you do not need to keep looking at the book in the middle of your practice. It can be beneficial to touch each point when you run through them for the first time. Don't worry: If you forget a point while practicing, it is not a problem. Alternatively, you can make a recording of your voice saying each point and play it back to guide your meditation.

Observing Sensation

TIME: 20 MINUTES · TYPE: MODERN

For this meditation, it is essential that you first establish yourself as Awareness. If you're not familiar with knowing yourself as Awareness, it would be beneficial to start with the "What Am I?" meditation (see page 160) in chapter 8 before coming to this practice. This meditation is intended to bring non-dual recognition into the body as a lived and embodied experience.

1. Knowing yourself as Awareness, come to a comfortable seated posture.

2. With your eyes open or closed, notice sensation in your body. Be aware of your body's temperature, the texture of clothes on your skin, the bottoms of your feet, the space behind your ears and between your fingers, and the muscles around your eyes.

3. Take note of all sensations from Awareness as Awareness. Do not believe your mind when it tries to label some sensations as "good" and others as "bad." Acknowledge the mind's commentary, but come back to the simple, equanimous observation of sensation in the body.

4. Be aware of these sensations as varying degrees of vibrant energy. Some sensations appear as thick and condensed vibrations, and others are more open, spacious, and almost entirely empty of vibration.

5. Forget labels such as "arm," "leg," "hand," or "foot." Simply observe and witness sensations like clouds of vibration appearing within spacious Awareness. Like a child with a deep and humble curiosity, watch sensation as if for the first time.

6. If your body feels pulled to move and explore sensation in movement, allow it to, but do not get caught in the thought, "I am the body moving my arm." Instead, just notice the body's natural and intuitive way of moving. Be slow and gentle, and always rest as pure Awareness as you move through this practice.

7. Slowly open your eyes and become aware of your surroundings. Do not re-identify as the body alone. Know yourself as Awareness observing the natural and spontaneous unfolding of the vibrancy of life through form.

TIP: If this practice makes you feel ungrounded, frustrated, or disturbed in any way, try the "Shaking Meditation" (see page 84), followed by the "Alternate-Nostril Breathing" meditation (see page 78).

Body of Space

TIME: 15 TO 20 MINUTES · TYPE: MODERN

Part of the practice of Tantra is learning to disidentify with the varying attachments we have to the body, emotions, and thoughts. Disidentifying allows us to identify with the space of being beyond individuality instead and enter into the transcendent realm. This practice is drawn from the *Vijnana Bhairava Tantra*. It helps us let go of the body through a constructive process of imagining that the body is limitless and without boundaries.

1. Sit in a comfortable position, with your back straight and vertical. Sitting cross-legged or in the lotus position is best, but sitting in a chair is also good. If these positions are unavailable, you can lie down on the floor or in the grass.

2. Close your eyes, tilt your head up slightly, and bring your focus to the area of your throat. Begin to inwardly chant the mantra "ham" (pronounced as "hum"). Continue this for a few minutes.

3. Now imagine that your body is limitless, without boundaries. Move all around your body and perceive it without form and shape. Whichever way the mind might hang on to something, let it go.

4. Let the experience that springs forth be fully embraced. Allow your being, including your mind and energy, to fully dissolve into space.

5. When 15 minutes have passed, come slowly back into your mind, energy, and body, noticing the sensations throughout.

TIP: Performing the "Alternate-Nostril Breathing" practice (see page 78) before this meditation will help settle the mind. When you first try this meditation, you might find resistance or even fear (which arises from the fear of death) preventing you from fully embracing the experience. With time, it gets easier and more comfortable to enter into the so-called "spaceless space."

CHAPTER 6

MEDITATIONS TO CULTIVATE FREQUENCIES OF ENERGY

Many Tantrik lineages and paths involve work with and cultivation of energy. Energy practices often are preliminary and help awaken latent power. These practices can range from mantra to breath control (*pranayama*) to visualizations. Some practices also utilize energy to bring glimpses of the Ultimate. The use of energy-related methods connects us directly to Shakti. Although different mantras may be used for a variety of deities, ultimately Shakti is everything; therefore, she is in every deity. To successfully work with energy in any form, we need the blessings of Shakti.

Mantra for Chakra Purification

TIME: 20 MINUTES · TYPE: MODERN

In Tantra, chakras are fundamental structures of energy that, when unblocked, can bring more power into the Being and help raise Kundalini Shakti (see page 39). In the following meditation, you will focus on purifying each of the elements of the body (earth, water, fire, air, and space) and their corresponding chakras to bring balance to your system. This practice is best performed over a series of days, focusing on one chakra each day and moving from the muladhara (root) chakra upward until you reach the vishuddha (throat) chakra.

1. Find a comfortable seated position to practice in, with your spine straight and erect but relaxed. It's best to practice sitting cross-legged on the floor, as this aids the mind's focus. However, this meditation can also be done while sitting in a chair.

2. With your eyes open or closed, internalize your attention by bringing awareness to one of the chakras.

3. Take a breath. While exhaling, begin repeating the bija mantra of the element associated with the chakra you are focusing on today. Repeat the mantra at a steady and consistent pace that feels easy but not dull. The mantras are as follows:

- "lam" (for earth, which is related to the muladhara chakra)
- "vam" (for water, which is related to the svadisthana chakra)
- "ram" (for fire, which is related to the manipura chakra)
- "yam" (for air, which is related to the anahata chakra)
- "ham" (for space, which is related to the vishuddha chakra)

4. Take note of any sensations that come, and stay attentive to the chakra while also contemplating the element of the chakra. For example, when meditating on water and the svadisthana chakra, reflect on the feeling of water inside and outside of the body.

5. After 20 minutes, take a moment to recognize how this element is balanced within your system.

TIP: This process can purify the chakras, thereby readying the system for Kundalini Shakti, and should be performed for three months to a year.

Visualizing the Elements

TIME: 20 MINUTES · TYPE: MODERN

In Tantra, each element has a different symbol, and these symbols correspond to the subtle energies of the chakras. The earth is a square, water is a crescent moon, fire is an upward-pointing triangle, air is a circle, and space is an egg shape. These symbols relate to the unconscious part of the mind and, when contemplated (as in this meditation), can awaken the characteristics of the chakras within the practitioner. For example, contemplating the muladhara (root) chakra can bring steadiness and grounding to the Being.

1. Choose the element you would like to work with.

2. Draw or print the symbol of the element on a piece of paper around 8" x 11" in size. Place this drawing in front of you at eye level about an arm's length away.

3. Find a comfortable seated position to practice in, with your spine straight and erect but relaxed. Sitting cross-legged on the floor aids the mind's focus. However, you can also do this meditation while sitting in a chair.

4. Begin by bringing your attention to your third eye. Gaze softly up towards the area in the middle of your forehead for about five minutes.

5. Next, bring your gaze upon the symbol in front of you for about one minute.

6. Close your eyes and visualize this symbol with clarity while contemplating the element. Do this for one minute.

7. Repeat steps 5 and 6 for 10 minutes.

8. After 10 minutes, take a moment to become aware of any sensations within your body or mind. Become aware of how the element is now strong and balanced. Rest here for five minutes.

TIP: Be relaxed with yourself around the timing of this meditation. Allow things to flow spontaneously and trust your intuition.

Chakra Breathing

TIME: 15 MINUTES · TYPE: MODERN

In Tantra, the breath is intimately connected to the energy of the Being. In this practice, you will use the breath to help bring energy into the seven chakras. This method allows you to begin to feel arising energies in the different parts of your body, thereby bringing greater awareness to each of the chakras.

1. Sit in a comfortable position with your back straight. Sitting cross-legged is best, but sitting in a chair is good, too. You can even lie down.

2. Bring your attention to one of the chakras in the front of the body. You may place your hands in the area where the chakra resides.

3. Breathe in deeply through your nose. Imagine energy moving from your nostrils down to the chakra you're focusing on.

4. Stay focused on the chosen chakra while exhaling and imagine that the energy is expanding outward.

5. After 10 minutes, bring your awareness to the chosen chakra's corresponding location in the spine and notice a deepening of awareness.

6. After 20 minutes, allow yourself a moment to feel the sensations of the chakra.

TIP: This method is best performed by focusing on one chakra per day over a series of days. Move from the muladhara (root) chakra upward, day by day, until you reach the sahasrara (crown) chakra, which will take one week. Repeat this process to purify the chakras and thereby ready the system for Kundalini Shakti.

Shining Chakra Meditation

TIME: 15 MINUTES · TYPE: MODERN

This meditation visualizes each chakra as shining and radiant and moves energy from chakra to chakra, from the root to the crown. This practice will help you purify each chakra and better perceive the rising of energy.

1. Sit in a comfortable position, with your back straight and vertical. A cross-legged position is best, but sitting in a chair is fine if cross-legged is not possible.

2. Bring the focus of your awareness to the muladhara chakra. Then, with an inhalation, bring energy down to the perineum area and visualize that the chakra is shining with a bright, golden light. This light brings purification to the area; you may feel a slight vibration or vibrancy there.

3. Repeat step 2 with each chakra as many times as possible until the end of the meditation. The location of each chakra is as follows (see the diagram on page 40):

  - Muladhara: the perineum
  - Svadisthana: the pubic bone
  - Manipura: the navel
  - Anahata: the center of the chest, two to three finger-widths above the base of the sternum
  - Vishuddha: the middle of the throat
  - Ajna: the center of the forehead
  - Sahasrara: the very top of the head

4. At the end of the meditation, notice the energies ascending along the spine to the sahasrara chakra.

TIP: It is helpful to return to this meditation regularly. After practicing it for several weeks, begin focusing on areas in the spine at the horizontal level of each chakra. For example, for the muladhara chakra, the focus would shift from the perineum to the coccyx on the spine. This shift will deepen awareness.

Healing Mantra

TIME: 20 MINUTES · TYPE: TRADITIONAL

As a holistic science, Tantra teaches that in order to follow the Tantrik path, both the body and mind should be healthy and strong. The repetition of the mantra in this practice aligns your energies and awakens the chakras. It brings joyous feelings, sparks your body's healing force, and helps free you from the fear of death. Reciting this mantra when taking medicines can help maximize their potency, especially when those medicines are ayurvedic. You can also use this mantra to support the healing process for others.

1. Light a candle and place it at arm's length in front of you.

2. Find a comfortable seated position, preferably cross-legged on the floor. It is ideal to have an asana (a small mat) made of natural materials to sit on. This meditation can also be done in a chair.

3. Set an intention for the meditation. Take a moment to call upon your spiritual teachers, guides, ancestors, and anything else that uplifts you in a sacred way to give you support during this meditation.

4. With a straight back and a relaxed body, focus your attention on the ajna (third eye) chakra in the middle of your forehead. When this becomes comfortable, you can keep your focus there while you close your eyelids. Begin to repeat this mantra internally:

Aum tryambakam yajaamahe sugandhim pushtivardhanam.

Urvaarukamiva bandhanaan-mrityormuksheeya maamritaat.

5. Say this mantra with as much reverence and devotion as possible. If you are tired, you can repeat the mantra more quickly to bring wakefulness. If you are feeling restless and overwhelmed, try saying the mantra more slowly.

6. When you have finished, take a moment to feel the healing energies of the Divine flow through you.

7. Thank your spiritual teachers, guides, and ancestors.

8. If using an asana, fold it up and keep it somewhere it won't be handled or touched by anyone else.

TIP: The mantra translates as: "We worship the three-eyed One (Shiva), who nourishes all. Like the fruit falls from the bondage of the stem, may we be liberated from death and mortality." If you do not have the mantra memorized, it is okay to keep your eyes open and simply read it. Repeating the mantra while reading it will still bring you all of the benefits. This mantra should not be recited if you are postnatal or menstruating or if a death has recently occurred in your immediate family. This mantra creates an upward flow of energy, but at these times in our lives the energy naturally flows in a different direction and should not be disturbed.

Mantra for Overcoming Obstacles

TIME: 20 MINUTES · TYPE: TRADITIONAL

In Tantra and other Hindu traditions in India, people often turn to Lord Ganesha, also known as Ganapataye, the overcomer of obstacles, for support when they face problems. This mantra helps connect you to the energy of Ganapataye in order to clear obstacles, whether mundane or spiritual, that can keep you from living a healthy life or performing sadhana.

1. Light a candle and place it at arm's length in front of you.

2. Find a comfortable seated position, preferably cross-legged on the floor. It is ideal to have an asana (a small mat) made of natural materials to sit on. This meditation can also be done in a chair.

3. Set an intention for the meditation, making sure to list obstacles you wish to overcome. Take a moment to call upon your spiritual teachers, guides, ancestors, and anything else that uplifts you in a sacred way to give you support during this meditation.

4. With a straight back and a relaxed body, focus your attention on the ajna (third eye) chakra in the middle of your forehead. When this becomes comfortable, you can keep your focus there while you close your eyelids. Begin to repeat this mantra internally:

om gam ganapataye namaha

5. Say this mantra with as much reverence and devotion as possible. If you are tired, you can repeat the mantra more quickly to bring wakefulness. If you are feeling restless and overwhelmed, try saying the mantra more slowly.

6. When you have finished, take a moment to feel the energies of Ganapataye flowing through you, bringing a sense that you will overcome all obstacles in your way.

7. Thank your spiritual teachers, guides, and ancestors.

8. If using an asana, fold it up and keep it somewhere it won't be handled or touched by anyone else.

TIP: This mantra translates as: "Salutations to Ganapataye, who is the overcomer of all obstacles." Instead of reciting it for 20 minutes, you can recite it 27, 54, or even 108 times. This mantra should not be recited if you are postnatal or menstruating or if a death has recently occurred in your immediate family.

Mantra for Courage and Protection

TIME: 20 MINUTES · TYPE: TRADITIONAL

Ferocity, courage, and the ability to overcome limitations are important qualities for a sadhak to cultivate. This practice will connect you with the energy of the Goddess Durga, who is fierce, protects us like a mother would her young, and brings courage to her devotees.

1. Light a candle and place it at arm's length in front of you.

2. Find a comfortable seated position, preferably cross-legged on the floor. It is ideal to have an asana (a small mat) made of natural materials to sit on. This meditation can also be done in a chair.

3. Set an intention for the meditation. Take a moment to call upon your spiritual teachers, guides, ancestors, and anything else that uplifts you in a sacred way to give you support during this meditation.

4. With a straight back and a relaxed body, focus your attention on the ajna (third eye) chakra in the middle of your forehead. When this becomes comfortable, you can keep your focus there while you close your eyelids. Begin to repeat this mantra internally:

    om dum durgayei namaha

5. Say this mantra with as much reverence and devotion as possible. If you are tired, you can repeat the mantra more quickly to bring wakefulness. If you are feeling restless and overwhelmed, try saying the mantra more slowly.

6. When you have finished, take a moment to feel the healing energies of the Divine flow through you.

7. Thank your spiritual teachers, guides, and ancestors.

8. If using an asana, fold it up and keep it somewhere it won't be handled or touched by anyone else.

TIP: This mantra translates as: "Salutations to the great Goddess Durga, who is kind to the seekers of Truth and frightening to those who live in ignorance." It should not be recited if you are postnatal or menstruating or if a death has recently occurred in your immediate family.

Enlightenment Mantra

TIME: 20 MINUTES · TYPE: TRADITIONAL

In Tantra, a large part of the practice is about connecting with the Absolute Self. This mantra helps join you to the Higher Self through the energy of Naranaye, who is a form of the Divine bringing ultimate rest to the Being, or in other words, enlightenment.

1. Light a candle and place it at arm's length in front of you.

2. Find a comfortable seated position, preferably cross-legged on the floor. It is ideal to have an asana (a small mat) made of natural materials to sit on. This meditation can also be done in a chair.

3. Set an intention for the meditation. Take a moment to call upon your spiritual teachers, guides, ancestors, and anything else that uplifts you in a sacred way to give you support during this meditation.

4. With a straight back and a relaxed body, focus your attention on the ajna (third eye) chakra in the middle of your forehead. When this becomes comfortable, you can keep your focus there while you close your eyelids. Begin to repeat this mantra internally:

om namo narananaye

5. Say this mantra with as much reverence and devotion as possible. If you are tired, you can repeat the mantra more quickly to bring wakefulness. If you are feeling restless and overwhelmed, try saying the mantra more slowly.

6. When you have finished, take a moment to feel the energies of Naranaye flow through you, bringing peacefulness and connection to the Self.

7. Thank your spiritual teachers, guides, and ancestors.

8. If using an asana, fold it up and keep it somewhere it won't be handled or touched by anyone else.

TIP: This mantra translates as: "I bow to the Eternal within." Instead of reciting this mantra for a specific amount of time, you can recite it 27, 54, or even 108 times. It should not be recited if you are postnatal or menstruating or if a death has recently occurred in your immediate family.

Inner OM Mantra

TIME: 15 MINUTES · TYPE: TRADITIONAL

In many of the different traditions of India, the mantra OM or AUM has colossal importance. It is considered one of the most fundamental mantras in Indian spirituality. The practice described here of inwardly chanting the mantra comes from the *Vijnana Bhairava Tantra*. It links the breath with the mantra, raising Consciousness towards and beyond the sahasrara (crown) chakra, which brings inner contentment and peace.

1. Sit in a comfortable position, with your back straight and vertical. A cross-legged position is best, but sitting in a chair is good, too.

2. Bring your attention to the middle of your chest and take a few deep breaths, focusing there.

3. There are four different parts to this mantra that are each chanted separately and silently. They are as follows:

   a. On an exhalation, begin the inward chanting of this mantra with the letter "A" ("aw"). Focus on your chest.

b. With the letter "U" ("ew"), allow the energy to raise your awareness to the vishuddha (throat) chakra.

c. With the letter "M," bring the energy and focus to the ajna (third eye) chakra. Allow a prolonged "M" sound to move upward, becoming quieter and quieter in your mind, until your focus reaches beyond your head and up past the sahasrara (crown) chakra.

d. Take a moment to acknowledge the silence that is the sahasrara chakra as you inhale and begin this process again.

4. Silently repeat this mantra with awareness and focus. At the end of each repetition, allow your entire being to disappear into emptiness.

5. After 20 minutes, give yourself time to be present with what is happening in your mind, body, and spirit. Notice the subtle and vast silence beyond the physical, mental, and emotional world.

TIP: You may also choose to practice by chanting this mantra out loud (see "The OM Mantra," page 72), which is a great way to purify your surroundings.

Moving Breath

TIME: 20 MINUTES · TYPE: TRADITIONAL

This practice uses a mantra to help contemplate the two points of void in the Being. This helps you enter into the void, presence, and the Absolute. The mantra *hamsah* means "I am that." It refers to the "that-ness" of the Absolute, the uniting of Shakti with Shiva. During this practice, we contemplate this union and completeness.

1. Find a comfortable seated position to practice in, with your spine straight and erect but relaxed. The preferred position is cross-legged on the floor, as it aids the mind's focus. However, this practice can also be done while sitting in a chair.

2. Begin by bringing your attention to the breath in the middle of your chest. It might be helpful to place your hands over your chest to bring awareness here. Do this for one to two minutes.

3. Next, bring your awareness and attention outside of your body at the chest level. Focus here for one to two minutes.

4. Connect the breath with these two points and begin inwardly chanting the mantra "ham" (pronounced "hum"). Follow the breath to the middle of your chest. On exhalation, follow the breath outside of your body to the location in front of your chest, repeating the mantra "sah." When "sah" is pronounced, allow it to be extended with awareness disappearing into emptiness.

5. At the two points in and outside the chest, contemplate the void and the stillness of your Universal Being.

6. After 20 minutes, take a moment to be aware of any sensations within your body or mind and notice a profound calmness in the Being.

TIP: This practice can be done at any time of the day in any position, even while walking.

CHAPTER 7

MEDITATIONS TO AWAKEN THE HRIDAYA (HEART)

In Tantra, there are many points on the body that are very useful for sadhana, but the most critical point is called the hridaya, which is in the center of the chest. This point is known as the "seat of consciousness." In the West, we would call it the "Heart," not referring to the organ but to a spiritual Heart, as mystical traditions named it. Bringing your attention to this point carries forward love and all of its many qualities. Deepening into this point creates a connection to the Divine and immerses you in the space of silence and stillness. Without being distracted by thought, you can merge and become Universal Consciousness.

Gratitude Meditation

TIME: 5 TO 15 MINUTES · TYPE: MODERN

Gratitude is the key to opening the heart and developing humility. This meditation aims to cultivate gratitude and extend it to all beings everywhere. In a traditional Tantrik context, gratitude is necessary for honoring the teachings and the teacher (guru) at the end of any practice.

1. Find a comfortable seated position to practice in, with the spine straight and erect but relaxed. The preferred position is cross-legged on the floor, as it aids the mind's focus. However, you can sit in a chair instead if that is more comfortable. You can close your eyes or leave them gently open for this practice.

2. Begin by bringing your attention to the breath in the middle of your chest. It might be helpful to place your hands over your chest to bring awareness here. Do this for one to two minutes.

3. Think of something that you are thankful for and bring this feeling into your heart.

4. Allow this feeling of thankfulness to radiate beyond yourself, towards your family, close friends, acquaintances, neighbors, enemies, and all beings everywhere. Do not forget to send gratitude towards the teachings (*dharma*), the teachers (gurus), and the spiritual community (*sangha*).

5. If your mind wanders during the practice, be patient and focus on steps 3 and 4.

6. After 5 to 15 minutes, take a moment to be aware of a deep sense of gratitude towards all beings everywhere.

TIP: This practice is good for any time of the day, or even multiple times a day. It can be done in a short, five-minute session or over a longer period of time, depending on how busy you are. A moment before or after sleep and during a meal are excellent times to cultivate gratitude.

"I Am" Meditation

TIME: 15 TO 20 MINUTES · TYPE: MODERN

In Tantra, one of the quickest ways to awaken to your divinity is to connect to the most profound sense of the very feeling of existence. In this meditation, you will work with the mantra "AHAM," which means "I am." However, rather than reciting it over and over, you will use it to bring yourself back to presence whenever you notice your mind wandering.

1. Find a comfortable seated position to practice in, with your spine straight and erect but relaxed. The preferred position is cross-legged on the floor, as it aids the mind's focus. However, you can sit in a chair instead if that is more comfortable, or you can even lie down. You can close your eyes or leave them gently open for this practice.

2. Begin by taking some deep breaths. Focus on the middle of your chest, letting go of any tension in your body. Do this for one to two minutes.

3. Allow the breath to slow down and become light and natural. Maintain your awareness in the middle of your chest.

4. After a few minutes, slowly begin to say the mantra "AHAM" while bringing the mind back to the heart. Allow your focus to reside there. Any time you notice that your mind or feeling of centeredness strays from the heart, repeat this mantra.

5. Continue like this, sinking deeper and deeper into the heart. Notice that external sounds and even thoughts begin to move towards the heart. The heart becomes like a vortex.

6. After 10 to 15 minutes, slowly come back, with gratitude in your heart and a sense of presence and connection with the Universal.

TIP: In the beginning, it might seem challenging to connect with the heart. However, with persistence and practice, it will become much easier.

Everywhere the Heart of Shiva

TIME: 20 MINUTES · TYPE: TRADITIONAL

The Tantrik philosopher Abhinavagupta tells us that if we can see both friend and foe equally as Bhairava (a form of Shiva), we will then come to realize that everything in the manifest is Shiva. Having a unitary perception of the world like this brings profound joy and richness into our lives. It eliminates all suffering and frees us from the restraints of the mind.

1. Find a comfortable seated position. Let your shoulders, jaw, and belly relax deeply. Encourage your body to relax by taking some big inhalations and exhalations.

2. When you feel like your body has come into a calm state of being, take a few deep breaths into the center of your chest. Take a moment to connect with the heart and really land in this sacred space.

3. With your eyes closed, visualize someone whom you love very deeply. Visualize them standing or sitting about six feet away from you.

4. Send blessings and love out to them, radiating from your heart with each breath. Send them all of your love, prayers, and kindness with the most profound humility and, with the utmost reverence, acknowledge that they are the Divine embodied. Spend about three minutes here.

5. Feel love radiating from them back towards you. Feel that you are equal in your divinity and united in compassionate kindness. Bathe in the powerful space of love that is forming between the two of you. Spend about three minutes here.

6. When you feel established in this love, allow the visualization to fade, but keep this sense of love shining out from your chest.

7. Bring forward the image of an acquaintance or someone you barely know. See them standing or sitting six feet away from you. Repeat steps 4 and 5.

8. Allow the image of the acquaintance to fade, but keep this loving energy flowing.

9. Visualize a foe or someone you hold grievances towards standing or sitting six feet away from you. Repeat steps 4 and 5. Know that this part of the meditation can be quite difficult and requires patience, persistence, and practice.

10. Drop all visualizations and spend the last few minutes of the meditation resonating in your own heart space. Be careful not to get into your mind. Do not analyze why some beings are more challenging to love than others. Do not ruminate on past grievances. Simply notice and breathe into the living space that surrounds you. Recognize that as you go about your day, there is an opportunity to meet each being you encounter with this same humble, loving reverence.

TIP: Know that it is very natural to find it more and more difficult to keep giving and receiving love as you move through this meditation. Move gently and have patience with yourself.

Heart Kriya

TIME: 10 MINUTES · TYPE: MODERN

In Tantra yoga, it is understood that there are five sheaths, or layers, to the human being. The heart also has five layers. *Kriya* means "action"; the Heart Kriya is a physical practice you can perform to open up the many layers of the heart.

1. Come into a kneeling position on the ground, with your hands in a prayer mudra over the heart in the center of your chest. For the prayer mudra, bring the palms of your hands together with fingers extended.

2. With your eyes open or closed, take a moment to breathe into your heart space and bring your awareness down into the heart. Allow your breath to encourage your body and mind to come into a peaceful state of being. Find silence and stillness merely by resting in this prayer position.

3. From the peaceful silence, allow a prayer, intention, or compassionate blessing to rise out of your heart. You may give it words, you may feel it, or you may even visualize it. Allow the prayer to arise in whatever way feels comfortable and natural for you.

4. Feel the prayer developing in your heart. Feel as though it is accumulating behind the heart and in your hands (in prayer mudra).

5. On your next inhalation, push your prayer mudra and your internal prayer up overhead and rise higher onto your knees. Open your arms wide and push the heart up towards the sky with a slight backbend.

6. On your exhalation, bring your hands back together in prayer mudra overhead, then slowly lower them to the heart. At the same time, come back down into your original kneeling position.

7. Inhale as you rise, and exhale as you bring your hands back to prayer mudra. On the inhalation, feel as though you are offering your devotion to the Universe. On the exhalation, feel as though you are receiving the blessings of the prayer in your heart.

8. Repeat steps 5 through 7 for several minutes.

9. On your final exhalation, rest in your kneeling position with your hands at the heart center in prayer mudra. Bow your head slightly in reverence to your heart. Take a moment to reflect on how your perspective has changed since you first started the practice. How are you feeling physically, mentally, and emotionally? Take a few final breaths into the heart. Trust that your prayers have been received.

TIP: If kneeling is not comfortable for you, feel free to modify this practice. You can do it sitting in a chair or cross-legged on the ground. In these positions, you will stay seated as you inhale and raise your hands overhead.

Merging with the Hridaya

TIME: 5 TO 20 MINUTES · TYPE: TRADITIONAL

Many of us live disconnected from our hearts. In Tantra, the hridaya is the heart of Shiva; it is the seed from which all of life sprouts. To live disconnected from the heart is to live disconnected from our source. This effortless practice will cultivate pratyahara (a withdrawal of the senses) as you focus on the physical heart. As the senses fade, you will dissolve into deeper aspects of the heart and eventually land in the silent, seamless source of our eternal Being.

1. This meditation can be done anywhere, even while sitting on the bus or waiting for dinner to cook. However, when you first begin practicing, it may be easier to do this meditation while sitting in a formal meditative position.

2. Close your eyes or find a soft gaze. Take a moment to allow your body to soften and relax. Get out any final adjustments, until you feel that you've found a place where you can be comfortable.

3. Breathing through your nose, inhale and exhale deeply several times.

4. Notice how as you take these deep breaths, your chest and the area of your heart rises and falls.

5. Notice how with each inhalation and exhalation, your awareness of the heart grows stronger. This awareness may come in the form of a visualization for some, while others may feel increasing sensations in the heart area.

6. Slowly allow your breath to become soft, regular, and natural. Keep your attention on the heart.

7. If thoughts come or distractions arise, remember that they are not a problem. Notice the distractions. They do not need to stop, but you must continue to focus your attention on the center of your chest.

8. Stay here for some time, drawing your attention deeper into the space of the heart.

9. When you're ready, open your eyes, slowly move your body, and go about your day.

10. As you move through the activities of the day, remember that you can return to this space simply by breathing into the heart.

TIP: If you have difficulty connecting with your heart, try placing one hand over it.

The Altar of the Heart

TIME: 5 TO 20 MINUTES · TYPE: MODERN

Many of us find that when we sit down to meditate, the mind becomes hostile and overwhelming. This meditation is a beautiful way to bring the mind into the heart. The heart is a silent temple residing in the center of our being. Remember that the physical heart can be used as a gateway into the supreme heart of Shiva. As the mind and thoughts disintegrate, we are left in the peace of our being.

1. Find any comfortable position. This could be sitting on the floor or in a chair or even lying on the ground. If you choose to lie down, resist falling into sleep during the meditation.

2. Close your eyes and focus your attention on the silence of the heart.

3. As you rest here, expect that your mind will begin to become agitated. As thoughts come, imagine that you are plucking them out of your mind and pulling them down into your heart. As they're brought down, they dissolve into the potency of the silence of the heart.

4. Return again to resting in the silent spaciousness that is the nature of the heart. Thoughts, emotions, or sensations may arise that will distract you from the silence. Notice these distractions and lovingly offer them to the altar of the heart.

5. Feel how when offered lovingly, anything will be accepted by your heart and transformed into silence.

6. Through consistent practice, you will begin to find that you're able to spend longer and longer resting in the silence of the heart.

7. Continue for some time. When you're ready, slowly open your eyes.

8. Close with a moment of gratitude.

TIP: Know that your heart loves to receive offerings. Know that nothing is "bad" or "good" in the realm of the heart. Any offering given with reverence and respect is the perfect gift for the heart.

The Eyes of the Heart

TIME: 10 TO 20 MINUTES • TYPE: MODERN

For many of us, our sense of self exists behind the eyes and within the mind. However, when we view the world solely from the mind, we cannot see the infinite possibility that life has to offer us. Instead, we are controlled by the mind's attachments and aversions and cannot reach our full potential. In this simple meditation, you will drop this identification down into the heart and attempt to see the world from there instead. When we live from the heart, we are intimately connected with all of life's possibilities, we are unbound by the tethers of the mind, and we are free.

1. Settle into a comfortable position and become aware of your state of being. Notice your mind's inner commentary about your day, your relationships, your activities, and so on.

2. Drop your attention down into your heart. Take a moment to center yourself there. This can be done in any way that feels natural for you. Feel as though your True Self resides here. This sacred space in the center of your chest is the source of your being. Take 5 to 10 minutes to settle into this space.

3. With your eyes closed, notice sounds around you. How does it feel to hear from the space of the heart? Notice sensations on your skin. How does it feel to observe sensation from the space of the heart? Keeping your eyes closed, allow your attention to move through each of the senses other than sight. Spend 5 to 10 minutes noticing taste, touch, smell, and sound from the heart.

4. Slowly open your eyes, taking in all of the colors and shapes that surround you. How does it feel to see the world from the heart? If you feel your identification moving back up towards the mind's commentary, close your eyes and re-center in the heart.

5. When you are finished, get up and go about your day but continue to witness every experience from the space of the heart.

TIP: It may be helpful to place one hand over the center of your chest as you practice to help ground yourself into the heart space.

Expanding Heart Meditation

TIME: 5 TO 20 MINUTES · TYPE: MODERN

There is far more to the human being than the physical body. In this meditation, you will expand the heart through the simple combination of breath and focused attention. In this expansive state, the heart is open and becomes the space from which you can move, act, and relate in the world. Through consistent practice, this meditation can bring you to the non-dual recognition that the heart is the space within which all life unfolds.

1. This meditation can be done in a traditional meditative posture. However, if you have difficulty relaxing your body or connecting with your breath, you may find it more beneficial to do this practice while lying down.

2. Close your eyes and take a moment to connect with your breath. Allow it to become longer and deeper with each inhalation and exhalation.

3. Notice your breath running over your heart. Feel as though with each inhalation you connect with the heart and with each exhalation you shine it out into the world. Notice that with each exhalation, the heart space expands.

4. As you inhale, keep connecting with the center of your chest. As you exhale, feel the heart expanding further and further out into the world. At first, this expansion may be in the vicinity of your physical body. However, as it continues, it will grow into the room, your home, your country, the world, and finally beyond the phenomenal world.

5. Take some time to really establish the heart in this expansive state. It may take time and practice; be patient with yourself.

6. When you are ready, bring your attention back to your body. Wiggle your toes; feel the sense of your physical body on the floor. Gently open your eyes and acknowledge the world around you.

7. Take a moment to recognize that your awareness is back in the physical world and that you are fully inhabiting your body. However, notice that your heart is still open, expansive, and all-encompassing.

TIP: If you choose to lie down in this meditation and you'd like to ensure you do not fall asleep, try meditating with your eyes open.

Divinity Dancing

TIME: 10 MINUTES · TYPE: MODERN

Many consider prayer to be something that is done formally, within the mind only, as if we're bartering with the Divine and making negotiations. However, true prayer is spontaneous and from the heart. It can help to practice this meditative prayer in a space that inspires and feels sacred to you, like a forest, a river, an altar, or a temple.

1. In a standing position, bring your feet about hip-width apart, with a little bend in your knees. Lengthen up through the spine. Let your shoulders fall away from your ears and take a few big breaths. You can close your eyes or leave them open with a soft gaze.

2. As you inhale, feel that you're pulling vital energy up through the soles of your feet into your body. As you exhale, feel that you're releasing all that no longer serves you. Repeat this for one to two minutes.

3. Internally, feel gratitude for all of your teachers, ancestors, family, and friends. Feel gratitude for the earth that supports you, the water that nourishes you, and the air that keeps you fresh. Feel gratitude for your breath, your body, and your heart. Bring your hands over your heart space and breathe into this gratitude.

4. Humbly set the intention that you may be able to drop the mind and offer dance as a prayer for the Divine, that the infinite may flow through you and express itself in blissful movement.

5. Allow your mind to fall away and let your body move as an offering or prayer for the Absolute. It does not need to be choreographed or artistic. It is preferable to do this without music. Let your breath be the song and let your body flow without inhibitions, moving with an open heart.

6. As you bring the dance to a close, place your hands over your heart and bow your head in reverence to the divinity within. Acknowledge that this divine spark is always within you and can be called upon at any time.

TIP: If you're having difficulty with this meditation, try starting with the "Gratitude Meditation" (see page 126) to help open the heart.

Hridaya Akasha

TIME: 20 MINUTES · TYPE: TRADITIONAL

Meditating on the sacred gateway of the hridaya in the center of the chest can lead us from personal Consciousness to transpersonal Consciousness. To make this transition is to move beyond your personal fears, anxieties, and limitations into the boundless possibilities of our infinite self. The more you can come to rest in the hridaya, the more you will transcend your ego and identify as Shiva Consciousness.

1. Find a comfortable resting posture. Close your eyes and take a few breaths to encourage your body to soften.

2. Bring your attention down into the center of your chest.

3. Feel as though there is a space in the center of your chest that leads to an infinite, expansive nothingness. Focus your attention on this space. Notice how with each breath, your attention falls deeper into this endless space.

4. Allow your breath to be soft, subtle, and natural. Keep resting your attention gently on this sacred space.

5. Thoughts, emotions, and sensations will come. Notice them, then bring your mind's eye back to the space in the center of your chest.

6. Although rationally you may know that your heart is still its normal size, the more that you bring your attention to this space, the more expansive it will feel. Rest in this space while doing absolutely nothing.

7. Slowly, bring movement into your fingers and toes. Take a big inhalation and a big exhalation. As you open your eyes and become aware of the "external world," notice that the infinite heart is ever-present and all-encompassing.

TIP: While the other meditations in this chapter connect you with the heart and center you there, this practice allows you to go into the deeper aspects of the Heart, merging with the Divine and becoming one with it. Therefore, it is best to gain experience with the other meditations in this chapter before coming to this one. We would specifically recommend practicing the "Merging with the Hridaya" meditation (see page 134) beforehand.

CHAPTER 8

MEDITATIONS FOR REALIZING NON-DUALITY

For many spiritual traditions in the Indian subcontinent, the endpoint is the realization of Absolute Awareness. This transcendental concept is indescribable but can be understood as your essential self beyond both time and space. To come to the recognition of Absolute Awareness is to come into non-duality, which is to go beyond the judgmental, comparative mind.

In Tantra, however, the endpoint lies in bringing this transcendental realization into an embodied understanding. The Tantrik does not remove themselves from the world, but rather learns to share their understanding so that love, compassion, and selfless service can flourish.

The meditations in this chapter are more advanced than those in earlier chapters. It may be beneficial for beginners to spend some time in earlier chapters building focus and energy and realizing the heart before coming to these practices. That said, it can also be nice to pair these meditations with some of the earlier meditations.

The Source of Sound

TIME: 15 MINUTES · TYPE: TRADITIONAL

Nada Yoga is the practice of using sound to come to the source of your being. The ancient Tantrik texts state that by keeping your attention focused on sound, you can perceive that all sounds rise out of the infinite and dissolve back into the infinite. Through this practice, you are absorbed in the infinite.

1. You will first need to find a piece of music to listen to. An Indian raga, Tibetan singing bowl recordings, or other peaceful, meditative music is recommended. Try to find a song that is at least 10 minutes long.

2. Find a comfortable position for your body to rest in. Many people practice this meditation in a formal meditative posture; however, it can also be practiced while lying down.

3. With your eyes closed, relax and soften your body. Encourage your shoulders to fall away from your ears and allow your jaw to release. Soften the muscles around your eyes and breathe deeply into your belly.

4. When you feel you have come into a space of presence and gentleness, begin to play the piece of music you have selected.

5. Listen intently to the layers of sound in the music. You do not need to label the different instruments or sounds. Simply notice the variety of sounds that you are experiencing. Allow your personal story and identity to fall away. Know only the sounds, and identify as the sounds.

6. If your mind wanders, bring it back to the sounds in the music. Feel as though this music is your whole existence. Be very attentive to the moment that sound begins and the moment that sound ends. Follow the sounds from beginning to end for the entirety of the song. You begin and end with each sound.

7. When the song ends, be attentive to the expansive, infinite silence, which is the container for and source of all sound. Rest in the vibrancy of this deep, endless silence. Remember that you are the beginning, the end, and the source of all.

TIP: Make sure you practice this meditation in a peaceful place where there will be no disruptions. It can be quite unsettling if someone makes a loud and unexpected noise when you have dropped so deeply into the sense of sound.

Gap between Thoughts

TIME: 20 MINUTES · TYPE: MODERN

In the spiritual traditions of India, including Tantra, it is understood that there is more to the human being than physical reality and that the mind stops us from seeing the infinite nature of the Reality of the Divine. Thus, many practices bring us a quietude of the mind. This adapted Tantrik practice uses thought as a tool to find the gap between thoughts, which is a place of no-mind and brings the possibility of seeing Reality.

1. Find a position on the floor or in a chair that is comfortable. Make sure that your back is straight yet relaxed.

2. Close your eyes and bring your attention to your breath. Allow it to slow down and become light. Keep your attention in the middle of your chest and let your body become relaxed. Do this for two to four minutes.

3. As you notice your mind entering a calm state, be aware of thoughts as they arise.

4. Notice how the mind operates. There are thoughts, but they do not always run successively. Instead, there are often spaces or gaps between them.

5. Try to be aware of the gaps between thoughts. As you bring your awareness to these gaps, you'll begin to have less and less attachment to thoughts and see more into the field of awareness.

6. After 15 minutes, bring yourself out of meditation. Allow yourself to rest in presence for a couple of minutes with your eyes open.

TIP: If you find that your thoughts are scattered and difficult to focus on, you might find it helpful to start this meditation with either the "Body Awareness" practice (see page 86) or "Alternate-Nostril Breathing" practice (see page 78).

Body without Support

TIME: 20 MINUTES · TYPE: TRADITIONAL

The mind and body are interconnected. So, if you deconstruct one, you end up also deconstructing the other. In this meditation from the *Vijnana Bhairava Tantra*, we visualize and feel that the body is without support. This frees the mind from thought constructs, allowing it to enter into Vast Empty Awareness.

1. Find a comfortable seated posture that supports your back and legs. You can also perform this meditation lying down on a bed in a very relaxed position.

2. Close your eyes and bring your attention to your breath in the middle of your chest. Start with a few deep breaths, inhaling fully and exhaling fully.

3. After a couple of minutes, when you feel deeply relaxed, begin to visualize that your body is without support. There is no floor, no bed, no chair beneath you—nothing.

4. Allow this visualization to become intensely and profoundly real. See that there is nothing around you, only endless space.

5. After some time, begin to notice that the mind has also become empty and without support. At this point, it stops being a container for samskaras (mental habits).

TIP: If you're feeling restless and unable to calm down the mind by step 3, feel free to do the "Alternate-Nostril Breathing" practice (see page 78) or the "Body Awareness" practice (see page 86).

Burning Body

TIME: 20 MINUTES · TYPE: TRADITIONAL

In Tantra, time is a concept of the mind known as Kala, the great destroyer of the manifested realm. In this meditation originating from the *Vijnana Bhairava Tantra,* we bring our attention to the process of time and visualize the body being burned to ashes. This method displaces the feeling of body and mind, bringing recognition of self and a profound sense of peacefulness.

1. It is recommended that you practice this meditation while lying down. Find a comfortable position on your back. If needed, feel free to place a pillow under your head and a pillow or two under your knees.

2. Bring your attention to your breath and close your eyes. Allow your body to become completely relaxed and free from troubles and tension.

3. When you feel entirely relaxed, bring your attention to your body. Visualize that your body has begun to burn intensely.

4. Be aware that this process helps burn all impurities in mind, body, and energy.

5. Let this burning consume you entirely, until everything, including your mind and karma, has disintegrated.

6. After 15 minutes, come back slowly into your body, moving your fingers and toes. Notice a purification of your body and energy and a profound sense of peacefulness.

TIP: Make sure that you are not tired when you do this practice, as you may fall asleep. Instead, find a time in the day when you feel awake and energized. If you are feeling restless, you can perform the "Alternate-Nostril Breathing" practice (see page 78) or the "Body Awareness" practice (see page 86) before this meditation.

Becoming the Sky

TIME: 20 MINUTES · TYPE: MODERN

In Tantra, we utilize many methods to come to the full Realization of the Universal. In this unorthodox meditation, you will fix your unblinking gaze upon the clear sky, aiming to dissolve the mind into it and realize the Infinite Universal Reality. This practice is found in the *Vijnana Bhairava Tantra*, but it is also a standard methodology in traditional yoga called Trataka.

1. It is only possible to practice this meditation on a clear day with few or no clouds (so that you are able to look at the sky).

2. Find a comfortable position on the earth from which you can see the clear sky without obstruction. You can lie down on the earth or rest your back on something.

3. Bring your attention into the heart space (*hrdakasa*) while breathing softly. You may close your eyes as you do this.

4. After some time, when you feel relaxed, open your eyes and gaze towards the sky.

5. If possible, allow your gaze to be unwavering and unblinking.

6. Start by feeling your connection to the earth under your body, breathing in and out deeply. Come to feel that the earth, the sky, and the entire world breathe with you. Continue this feeling for some time.

7. Now let go of any feelings or thoughts, becoming unmoving in body, emotions, and mind. Surrender into the infinite space of the sky, the Universe, and the Universal.

8. If thoughts crop up, witness them as clouds moving through the sky. They are not you, for you are the vast empty infinite sky, endless without form. Continue to let go, not grasping at anything.

9. After 15 minutes or so, close your eyes, noticing waves of peacefulness overwhelming your entire being. Be grateful for the world and your loved ones. Rest here in this space of gratitude until you're ready to get up.

TIP: You may notice your eyes either water or burn after some time. If this happens, feel free to close your eyes and move the practice into gazing softly into the sky.

Headlessness

TIME: 20 MINUTES · TYPE: MODERN

Often, while in the depths of meditation or as a result of a long-term sadhana, we feel that we are headless and that there is infinite space where the head once was. In this meditation, we explore this practice, using imagination creatively to bring about this result and deepen our state of awareness (see page 22).

1. Find a comfortable position. You can sit either in a chair or on the floor, with your back supported or not. Make sure that your back is straight and vertical yet relaxed.

2. Close your eyes and direct them towards your third eye in the middle of your forehead. Do this for five minutes. If this is difficult or if you feel dizzy, you can bring your gaze to the tip of your nose with your attention focused on the middle of your forehead.

3. When you start to have greater awareness or physical sensations in your third eye, bring your attention to the space above the back of your head.

4. Imagine that you are headless. Make this more than just a visualization. Instead, feel this and perceive that it is true.

5. If there are any thoughts or sense impressions in your mind, witness them as an observer and try not to engage with them. Instead, become more absorbed in the feeling of headlessness and the infinite space outside, above, and beyond you.

6. Continue this way until your Consciousness merges with the Universal, or until 15 minutes are up.

7. After the practice is finished, take a moment to continue feeling that you are headless, with your Consciousness free and peaceful.

TIP: If this meditation feels like "too much," discontinue the practice. Instead, do some of the grounding practices in chapter 6, especially the "Chakra Breathing" meditation (see page 108), focusing on your muladhara chakra. You can also use the "Alternate-Nostril Breathing" meditation (see page 78) to help ground you.

What Am I?

TIME: 20 MINUTES · TYPE: TRADITIONAL

In the *Vijnana Bhairava Tantra*, we are instructed to inquire, "What am I?" when there is no desire, no thought, and no activity. This question is probably as old as time itself, and it has been pondered in almost all of the major spiritual and philosophical traditions. This question and others like it have the power to bring you to Absolute Truth.

1. Find a comfortable position.

2. Take a moment to allow your system to settle. Close your eyes and use your breath to encourage your mind and body to release activity and disturbance. With each inhalation, feel a new peace coming into your system. With each exhalation, feel as though your mind and body are releasing and relaxing.

3. Notice that there is a stillness at the top and bottom of each inhalation and exhalation. There is a still moment in which you are neither inhaling nor exhaling. Become aware that, however small, this is a moment of inactivity. Inquire into this stillness, "What am I?" Rest here for some time.

4. Notice the thoughts in your mind. Recognize that although the mind may feel chaotic and hostile, there are still moments of spaciousness between thoughts. Witness thoughts as they appear, and notice how when we do not engage with them, they disappear. Inquire into this spaciousness, "What am I?" Thoughts come and go; you witness and inquire into the source of the "I." Stay like this, resting and inquiring into the spaciousness.

5. Recognize that you are free from desire when you rest in the stillness between breaths or the space between thoughts. There is a silence that is peaceful and content. Inquire into this silence, "What am I?"

6. Open yourself to perceive the silent, spacious stillness that is inherent in everything. These qualities are everywhere and nowhere in particular. Allow yourself to be wholly absorbed in this.

TIP: When inquiring, you do not need to ask, "What am I?" incessantly. Ask gently, listen, marinate, and experience the answer to this question in the silent, still spaciousness.

Resting as Awareness

On some days, this meditation can be significantly challenging; on others, it can be incredibly easy. If you notice yourself getting excited or disturbed by the "quality" of your meditation, simply remember that this is only your mind's interpretation and has no real weight or truth to it. Maintaining a state of equanimity and nonjudgment is integral to this meditation.

1. Bring your body into a comfortable position. This could be seated, lying on your back, or standing, whatever position works for you.

2. Take a few deep breaths and get any final squirms out of your body. Finally, bring your body into stillness.

3. As you inhale, say internally, "I am not the body." As you exhale, say internally, "I am not the mind." Repeat this for the next three to five minutes.

4. Bring the internal repetition to a close and allow the breath to be soft and natural. As thoughts, emotions, and sensations in the body arise, recognize that they are witnessed. You are the Awareness of whatever arises.

5. If you start to engage in thought or focus on sensations, gently bring the Awareness back to the pure perceiving of all. Thoughts and sensations come and go, but you remain aware of it all. Remain like this for 10 to 15 minutes, simply being aware.

6. As you bring the meditation to a close, feel peace in knowing that you are free from all disturbances of the mind and body as Awareness.

TIP: If you feel ungrounded after this practice, you can do the "Alternate-Nostril Breathing" practice (see page 78) or simply eat a nice, healthy meal and take a walk.

Aware of Awareness

TIME: 20 MINUTES OR LONGER · TYPE: TRADITIONAL

In the Tantrik tradition, it is essential to bring our "spiritual realizations" back into the world. We do not stay up on the mountaintop, nor do we draw a line between "spiritual life" and "human life." This meditation is meant to help you blur the two and experience an embodied non-dual understanding. Note that this is a secondary meditation to be performed following other preliminary practices.

1. Start with five minutes of the "Alternate-Nostril Breathing" practice (see page 78).

2. Spend five minutes doing the "Resting as Awareness" meditation (see page 162).

3. As you bring the "Resting as Awareness" meditation to a close, open and close your eyes. Ask yourself, "Am I more aware with my eyes open or closed? Or is it possible that I am equally aware in both situations?" Play with this inquiry for some time.

4. Slowly, bring some natural and spontaneous movements into your body. Allow these movements to come effortlessly and without force. This does not have to be beautiful or planned; just allow movement to come. Inquire, "Am I more or less aware as my body moves?" Contemplate and inquire.

5. Go about your day. Speak to your friends. Complete the tasks required of you. Continue to check in and ask, "Is Awareness here? Does anything that I come in contact with limit or inhibit Awareness?"

6. In the evening, as you lie down to sleep, be aware of Awareness drifting through the various states of awareness (see page 18).

TIP: If you forget to inquire throughout the day, do not be discouraged. Remember to as often as you can, and slowly this practice will become a healthy habit.

Locus of the Heart

TIME: 20 MINUTES · TYPE: MODERN

The Tantrik text the *Netratantra* teaches us that there are 16 sacred points on which one can meditate to localize the Self. In this meditation, you will gently move your attention between two of these holy points. This meditation helps bring peace and restoration to the body and mind. Through dedicated practice, it can expand your Consciousness until it becomes all-encompassing.

1. Find a comfortable meditative posture. Let your gaze be soft, or close your eyes and bring the gaze inside.

2. Invite your body to become strong in the spine and soft everywhere else.

3. Take a few moments to settle into the present moment. Breathe in and out through your nose. Notice thoughts, emotions, and sensations, but do not try to change what is present; simply notice.

4. With the body and mind settled, bring the attention towards the center of your chest. Become aware of a space in the area of the heart, one to two inches behind the sternum.

5. Once the attention can rest easy in this first space, bring it towards the second space, which is one to two inches in front of the chest. This space can be more challenging to find, as it is outside of your physical body. If you'd like, you can place a hand palm-up in this area and see if you can feel exhalations from your nose there. The place where breath and palm meet is where you will focus.

6. Now allow the attention to gently move back and forth between these two spaces inside and outside the body. On the inhalation, become aware of the inner space. On the exhalation, be mindful of the exterior space. Stay like this for some time. Keep the attention flowing across these two to four inches. Do not follow the breath up and out of the nostrils. Instead, imagine that the breath is merely traveling between these two spaces, as if you were breathing through your sternum.

>>

Continued

7. It is recommended that you practice up to step 6 for some weeks, or even months, before moving on to this step. Once you are naturally observing the breath flowing between these two spaces and your attention is firmly established, you can begin to inquire into this experience. Ask any questions about the nature of your existence that naturally arise. Alternatively, you can ask some of the following questions: "Is there really an inside and an outside of the body? Is the awareness of these two spaces inside, outside, both, or neither? When I'm aware of one locus, does the other cease to exist? Even if the inner space has more sensation, does that alone really make it more 'me'?"

TIP: See the section of this book on non-duality (see page 49) and the other non-dual meditations in this chapter for further support with step 7. This is a more advanced practice; it will be easier to perform once you have completed the meditations earlier in this chapter.

GLOSSARY

asana: The physical postures used during Tantrik practice; also meditation mats made of natural fabric.

Awareness: Also known as Absolute Awareness, this is not the awareness of sense perceptions, but instead the infinite and indivisible truth that permeates all existence. It is sometimes referred to as Consciousness, the True Self, the Self, Beingness, hridaya, or Shiva.

Ayurveda: An ancient healing methodology for the body and mind; can involve alternative medicines.

chakra: An energy center of the body where nadis intersect.

Consciousness: See Awareness.

diksha: The practice in which a Tantrik disciple receives initiation by an authentic guru.

Divine: Used to refer to the innate sacredness of life.

element: A building block of our physical universe.

enlightenment: Also known as *moksha*, this state is the highest goal of Tantra. When achieved, it brings liberation from the mind and self-knowledge as Absolute Awareness.

gunas: The three qualities—tamas, rajas, and sattva—that bind together the entire universe, including all that is tangible and intangible.

guru: A spiritual teacher who brings about Divine Awakening and enlightenment to spiritual seekers.

hatha yoga: A type of yoga that came from Tantra.

hridaya: Also known as "heart," this sacred entity is a person's deepest consciousness and the source of Shiva and Shakti. It does not refer to the physical heart or the anahata chakra.

jagrat: Also known as the waking state, this ordinary state occupies most of a person's life.

jiva: The individual soul of a living being.

Kundalini: A form of divine feminine energy (or Shakti) located at the base of the spine in the muladhara chakra.

Kundalini awakening: In this process, through regular spiritual practice, Kundalini energy can be awakened, after which it ascends through the body to the sahasrara chakra where Shiva resides, igniting Absolute Awareness.

manifest: The physical or material aspects of the Universe and the realms of energy, emotion, and thought.

mantra: A sacred word or group of syllables or sounds repeated during meditation to open cosmic energies and manifest the Divine within.

mudra: Gestures made by the hands, body, and sometimes mind during spiritual practice to bring forth different energies.

non-dualism: The perspective that holds that the Divine and the jiva are indivisible.

prana: The energy force of Shakti that creates and sustains all life.

sadhak: A practitioner of Tantra who brings about *siddhi* through spiritual practice.

sadhana: A spiritual practice such as meditation undertaken in order to change one's external or internal environment.

shaivite: A devotee of Shiva.

shakta: A devotee of Shakti.

Shakti: The activating energy of the Universe personified as the feminine aspect of the Divine.

Shiva: Consciousness and Awareness, existing beyond all space and time throughout the Universe, personified as the masculine aspect of the Divine.

siddhi: Perfecting one's spiritual practice so that clear and definable results are attained.

sushupti: Also known as the deep sleep state, this merging of the waking (jagrat) and dream (svapna) states does not allow for the perception of objects, experiences, concepts, or time.

svapna: In this state, also known as the dream state, the five senses are suspended and awareness travels out of the physical body into the mental-emotional body.

tantrika: A practitioner of Tantra who has been initiated by an authentic guru.

turiya: In this state, also known as the fourth state, a person transcends the day-to-day states of existence and experiences Absolute Awareness.

turiyatita: Also known as "perfection beyond the fourth"

state, this highest state of existence in Tantra is where Ultimate Reality is revealed.

Universe: The divinity that both surrounds and is held within us.

unmanifest: That which is formless and without structure or material in the Universe.

yantra: A sacred geometric symbol that represents the Divine.

yoga nidra: A state of awareness known as "conscious sleep" experienced between waking and sleeping.

RESOURCES

Shivoham Tantra and Guruji Maharaj

shivohamtantra.com

Guruji Maharaj, a master of Kundalini and authentic traditional Tantra, has guided hundreds of Indian and Western seekers through various sadhana processes to support their physical and spiritual wellbeing. He is the holder of the Shivoham Tantra Lineage under the guidance of Maha Guru Sri Bhairavananda.

Jean Klein

JeanKlein.WordPress.com

Jean Klein and the many students who have blossomed out of his teachings have been an incredible source of inspiration for Artemis and Bhairav. If you're interested in learning more about non-dual Tantra, look into the rich and powerful works and teachings of Jean Klein, Billy Doyle, Rupert Spira, Eric Baret, and Ellen Emmet.

The Himalayan Institute

HimalayanInstitute.org

The Himalayan Institute is an international nonprofit organization led by Tantrik teacher and lineage holder Pandit Rajmani Tigunait. It offers courses, trainings, and programs in yoga, meditation, spirituality, and holistic health online and in person.

The American Institute of Vedic Studies

VedaNet.com

The American Institute of Vedic Studies is run by David Frawley, an American Hindu teacher. Its website covers a wide range of topics relevant to this book, with excellent information on Tantrik spirituality.

REFERENCES

Avalon, Arthur. *The Serpent Power: The Secrets of Tantric and Shaktic Yoga*. New York, NY: Dover Publications Inc., 1974.

Britannica, T. Editors of Encyclopaedia. "Rigveda." *Encyclopedia Britannica*, March 12, 2020. Britannica.com/topic/Rigveda.

Dasgupta, Surendranath. *A History of Indian Philosophy*. Delhi: Motilal Banarsidass, 1975.

Doniger, Wendy, trans. *The Rig Veda: An Anthology: One Hundred and Eight Hymns, Selected, Translated and Annotated*. London: Penguin, 2005.

Feuerstein, Georg. *Tantra: The Path of Ecstasy*. Boston: Shambhala, 1998.

Finn, Louise M, trans. *Prapancasara Tantra: The Tantra on the Nature of Creation*. Bloomington, IN: Balboa Press, 2017.

Gyanshruti, Sannyasi, and Sannyasi Srividyananda. *Yajna: A Comprehensive Survey*. Munger, India. Yoga Publications Trust, 2006.

Khanna, Madhu, ed. *Thirty Minor Upanishads*. Translated by K. Narayanasvami Aiyar. New Delhi: Tantra Foundation, 2011.

Kinsley, David. *Tantric Visions of the Divine Feminine: The Ten Mahavidyas*. Delhi: Motilal Banarsidass, 2016.

Maharaj, Sri Nisargadatta. *I Am That: Talks with Sri Nisargadatta Maharaj*. Edited by Sudhakar S. Dikshit. Translated by Maurice Frydman. Durham, NC: The Acorn Press, 1988.

Mani, Vettam. *Puranic Encyclopaedia: A Comprehensive Dictionary with Special Reference to the Epic and Puranic Literature*. Delhi: Motilal Banarsidass, 1975.

The Mantra Mahodadhi of Mahidhara: English Translation by a Board of Scholars. Delhi: Sri Satguru Publications, 2002.

Mishra, Kamalakar. *Kashmir Saivism: The Central Philosophy of Tantrism.* Delhi: Sri Satguru Publications, 1999.

Mookerjee, Ajit. *Kundalini: The Arousal of the Inner Energy.* London: Thames & Hudson, 1982.

Nikhilananda, Swami, trans. *The Mandukya Upanishad with Gaudapada's Karika and Sankara's Commentary*, 1995.

Olivelle, Patrick, trans. *The Early Upanishads: Annotated Text and Translation.* Oxford: Oxford University Press, 1998.

Olivelle, Patrick, trans. *Upanisads.* Oxford: Oxford University Press, 2008.

Rama, Swami, Rudolph Ballentine, and Swami Ajaya. *Yoga and Psychotherapy: The Evolution of Consciousness.* Honesdale, PA: Himalayan Institute Press, 1976.

Saraswati, Swami Satyananda. *Yoga Nidra.* Yoga Publications Trust, 2002.

Saraswati, Swami Satyasangananda. *Sri Vijnana Bhairava Tantra: The Ascent.* Yoga Publications Trust, 2004.

Sastry, Alladi Mahadeva, trans. *The Taittiriya Upanishad: With the Commentaries of Sri Sankaracharya, Sri Suresvaracharya, Sri Vidyaranya.* Chennai, Tamil Nadu: Samata Books, 2007.

Singh, Jaideva, trans. *Vijnanabhairava, or Divine Consciousness: A Treasury of 112 Types of Yoga.* Delhi: Motilal Banarsidass, 1979.

Vasu, Rai Bahadur Srisa Chandra, trans. *The Shiva Samhita.* New Delhi: Munshiram Manoharlal, 1996.

INDEX

A
Abhinavagupta, 130–131

Absolute Awareness, 13, 18, 19, 23, 33, 37, 147

Ajna chakra (third eye chakra), 46, 60–61

Anahata chakra (heart chakra), 44

Asana mats, 26

Asana (postures), 25–26

Awareness, states of, 18–23

Ayurveda (healing methodology), 29

B
Bliss body (*anandamaya kosha*), 19

Body awareness, 86–87
  about, 37, 77
  Body of Space, 100–101
  Earthly Senses, 80–82
  Observing Sensation, 98–99
  Rocking Meditation, 88–89
  Shaking Meditation, 84–85
  Taste Meditation, 90–91
  Yoga Nidra, 94–97

Body of higher intellect (*vijnanamaya kosha*), 19

Breath awareness
  about, 37, 77
  Alternate-Nostril Breathing, 78–79
  Chakra Breathing, 108–109
  Moving Breath, 122–123
  Silent Breath, 92–93

Buddhist Tantra, 6

C
Chakras, 38–47
  Chakra Breathing, 108–109
  Mantra for Chakra Purification, 104–105
  Shining Chakra Meditation, 110–111

Citta (individual Consciousness), 48

Consciousness, 14

Cosmic Consciousness, 25

Courage mantra, 116–117

D
Dakshinachara (right-handed path), 9–10

Dancing meditation, 142–143

Das Mahavidyas (Ten Wisdom Goddesses), 9

Deep Sleep State (sushupti), 21

Diksha (initiation), 24, 27

Divine aspects, 7–9

Dream State (svapna), 20–21

Duality, 49. *See also* Non-duality realization

E
Elements, visualizing, 106–107

Emotional benefits, 31–32

Energetic body (*pranamaya kosha*), 19

Energy frequencies

about, 38, 103
Chakra Breathing, 108–109
Enlightenment Mantra, 118–119
Healing Mantra, 112–113
Mantra for Chakra
    Purification, 104–105
Mantra for Courage and
    Protection, 116–117
Mantra for Overcoming
    Obstacles, 114–115
Moving Breath, 122–123
Shining Chakra
    Meditation, 110–111
Visualizing the Elements,
    106–107
Enlightenment, 13
Enlightenment Mantra, 118–119

F

Focusing the mind
about, 36, 55
Bhairava Meditation, 70–71
Closing the Gates of
    Sensation, 66–67
Focusing on a Flame, 56–57
Focus on the Heart
    Center, 74–75
Meditating on the Third
    Eye, 60–61
Noticing the Gaps, 68–69
The OM Mantra, 72–73
Visualizing an OM
    Symbol, 58–59
Yantra-Drawing
    Meditation, 62–63
Yantra-Gazing
    Meditation, 64–65

Fourth State (turiya), 18–19,
    21–23

G

Gheranda Samhita, 60
Gratitude Meditation, 126–127
Gunas, 13–14
Gurus, 24, 27

H

Hatha Yoga Pradipika, 56
Hindu Tantra, 4, 6
Hridaya (heart) awakening
about, 48 125
The Altar of the Heart, 136–137
Divinity Dancing, 142–143
Everywhere the Heart of
    Shiva, 130–131
Expanding Heart
    Meditation, 140–141
The Eyes of the Heart, 138–139
Gratitude Meditation, 126–127
Heart Kriya, 132–133
Hridaya Akasha, 144–145
"I Am" Meditation, 128–129
Merging with the
    Hridaya, 134–135

I

"I Am" Meditation, 128–129
Ida nadi, 47
Inner OM Mantra, 120–121

J

Jiva (soul), 7

K

Kaula level, 11–12

ACKNOWLEDGMENTS

We want to acknowledge all the tantrikas who came before us and contributed in countless ways through their self-investigation to the knowledge that we have to share. Infinite gratitude to our Beloved Guruji Maharaj and Guruma, whose unconditional love holds us and supports us in all that we do.

This book would not have been possible without the incredible generosity of our dear friend Alisha J. Flecky, whose work and offerings we recommend. Some of the greatest gifts in our lives are our friends in the Anuttara sangha, especially Ishvari Olivia Belanger, whose tireless dedication to the school kept things afloat while we were writing this book. We want to thank our dear sangha brother Tomer Weiss as well for his selfless contributions. We are also incredibly grateful to the Nisga'a Lands, which hold and nourish us.

Thank you to Adrian Potts and Callisto Media for their support, patience, and kindness.

Thank you to our parents Susan English, Barry English, Brant Doyle, and Deirdre Quinn, who only ever supported our spiritual journeys into the weird and wonderful world of Tantra. Thank you to Rishi Fraser McDonald for being a light in our lives, to Bert Spisak, our special friend who continues to inspire us with his boisterous heart, and to all of the teachers and students who have come into our lives—you have made this happen.

ABOUT THE AUTHORS

Artemis Emily Doyle and **Bhairav Thomas English** are students and practitioners of various mystic traditions. They are lineage holders in the tradition of Shivoham Tantra. They live in a simple home off-grid in the sacred mountains of the Nisga'a people in northern British Columbia, Canada. Together they established Anuttara Ashram and the Anuttara Turiyatita School, which offer teachings and trainings in non-dual Tantra, Tantra yoga, and classical Tantra. They create spaces for love to take form through service, study, and spiritual practice. For Tantrik courses, articles, and inspiration, visit their website Anuttara.org.

CPSIA information can be obtained
at www.ICGtesting.com
Printed in the USA
LVHW010921231021
701215LV00001B/1